DERMO!

The REAL Russian Tolstoy Never Used

ZVER' MUZHIK
A sex machine.
(literally, "animal man.")

KAK ZHIZN'?
How's life?

KRYSHA POEKHALA
To go bonkers.
(literally, "the roof is sliding.")

NA KOI PES?
What the hell?
(literally, "on whose dog?")

STROIT' GLAZKI
To flirt.
(literally, "to build eyes.")

YA TEBYA LYUBLYU
I love you.

EDWARD TOPOL is one of Russia's best-selling novelists.

DERMO!

The REAL Russian Tolstoy

Never Used

Edward Topol

Translated by Laura E. Wolfson

Illustrations by Kim Wilson Brandt

A PLUME BOOK

PLUME
Published by the Penguin Group
Penguin Books USA Inc., 375 Hudson Street,
New York, New York 10014, U.S.A.
Penguin Books Ltd, 27 Wrights Lane,
London W8 5TZ, England
Penguin Books Australia Ltd, Ringwood,
Victoria, Australia
Penguin Books Canada Ltd, 10 Alcorn Avenue,
Toronto, Ontario, Canada M4V 3B2
Penguin Books (N.Z.) Ltd, 182–190 Wairau Road,
Auckland 10, New Zealand

Penguin Books Ltd, Registered Offices:
Harmondsworth, Middlesex, England

First published by Plume, an imprint of Dutton Signet,
a division of Penguin Books USA Inc.

First Printing, August, 1997
20 19 18 17 16 15 14 13 12

LIBRARY OF CONGRESS CATALOGING-IN-PUBLICATION DATA:
Topol, Edward.
    Dermo! : the real Russian Tolstoy never used / Edward Topol; translated by Laura E.
Wolfson; illustrations by Kim Wilson Brandt.
        p.   cm.
    ISBN 0-452-27745-0
    1. Russian language—Obscene words—Dictionaries—English. 2. Russian language—
Slang—Dictionaries—English. I. Title.
    PG2691.T67   1997
    491.73'21—dc21   97-12742
                                                                        CIP

Printed in the United States of America
Set in Minion
Designed by Leonard Telesca

Contents

Acknowledgments

The author thanks the publisher for the honor of presenting to an English-speaking readership the rich treasures and the soul of the great Russian language. The author also thanks translator Laura E. Wolfson, who in translating this book of Russian slang and swear words performed a most difficult task and successfully expressed the essence of the Russian soul in English. An enormous thanks to the editor Julia Serebrinsky for the care and attention she's given to this rather unladylike project.

Translator's Note

Reader beware: The verses that appear in this book in English translation accompanied by their Russian originals are *not* literal translations. Some liberties have been taken in order to achieve greater literary effect. Russian words presented in the Roman alphabet have not been transliterated according to any of the standard transliteration systems; priority has been placed on ease of pronunciation.

The translator wishes to thank GHK for his invaluable expertise and assistance with Cyrillic software during the translation of this book.

Introduction

I will now reveal to you the secret of Russian as spoken by real people.

But first, a brief introduction.

The great Russian author Ivan Turgenev, famous for his novel *Fathers and Sons*, his lyrical descriptions of the Russian countryside and his insights into the hearts and souls of Russian women, once proclaimed: "In time of doubt, in time of agonizing reflection, you have always been my mainstay and my hope, oh great and mighty Russian language! . . . There can be no doubt but that such a language was conferred upon a great people!" Ironically, Turgenev himself preferred to live in Paris with the French singer Paulina Viardot, a fact which people in Russia would rather overlook.

I have never heard the British say that English is a great and mighty language, nor do I recall ever hearing the French speak of the great French soul, but Russians tend toward gigantomania: Peter is Peter the Great, Catherine is Catherine the Great, Tolstoy is great, Stalin is great, Mother Russia is great, literature is great, snowfalls are never anything but great, and on the map of Russia there are twenty-four cities containing the word "great": Great Lip, Great Ruble, Great Digging, and Great Deafness, to name a few. It's worth noting that neither Paris nor Istanbul nor Tokyo call themselves "great cities," and yet here in Russia we find a place called "Digging" that is most definitely great, and its name alone reveals the secret ambitions of even the most provincial of Russian souls.

Of course, no one denies the greatness of Tolstoy and Dostoyevsky, but I have a feeling that in everyday life nineteenth century Russians never spoke like Turgenev's noble young heroines, Anna Karenina, or the brothers Karamazov, and if today someone were to stand up—in the Russian parliament or even at a Russian writers conference—and speak in the language of Tolstoy, people would think he was nuts.

The Russian language as it is taught in the most prestigious colleges in the West with reference to "great" Russian literature is as different from present-day speech in smell, taste, and potency as Evian water is from home brewed potato vodka.

This is why whenever I send off a new novel to be translated, I provide notes on every page of the manuscript explaining new words and slang expressions I use. Even professional translators, whose résumés include translations of the great Russian classics as well as serious contemporary works, do not know hundreds of words that make up contemporary Russian. These words are not included in the latest Russian version of spell check which is on my computer, so I enter these words into the memory myself. But then even if you memorize an entire dictionary of Russian curses and slang, you won't come close to *organic* Russian speech, if you don't know the main, or rather, the Great secret of the Russian language. And this is a secret I reveal to my translators in a note I always attach to the first page of the manuscript. It reads:

Dermo!

Dear Colleague! I will now reveal to you the secret of Russian as spoken by real people. Please remember it when you are translating all dialogues. I rely on this secret when writing dialogues and speeches for all my characters, from Gorbachev and Yeltsin right down to a prostitute plying her trade on Moscow's main drag. Here is the rule:

Every real Russian sentence is constructed so that the word "motherfucker" or "whore" can be inserted at any point—even after every word.

Only the translator's unfailing adherence to this rule can assure that the Russian characters' conversations and speeches will sound as if they are coming from the mouths of real people.

Flexibility is a trademark of Real Russian. In English, for example, words observe a certain etiquette and are placed in a sentence according to strict British norms of politeness (i.e., the predicate never elbows its way ahead of the subject and the verb always bows down in deference before His Majesty, the noun). Russian, on the other hand, emulates its homeland, where chaos generally rules, and the word order in a sentence is dictated by nothing more than how the speaker is feeling that day. This is why four-letter words can appear anywhere in a sentence and sound natural and even indispensable if the emotion calls for it. In English, the following sentence would sound extremely odd: "I, fuck, love, whore, you, bitch, so much!" Does that sound like any declaration of love you've ever heard? But if I write in Russian, "I love you so much!" it strikes a false note or sounds ironic to the Russian ear. To lend this exalted phrase the convincing note of genuine love, I have to let it go slumming, or as they say in Russian, let it sink down to the level of дерьмо (*der'mo*—shit) and write я, тебя, пала, так люблю! (*Ya, tebya, pala, tak lyublyu!*) that means literally "I, you, bitch, so much love!" or more idiomatically, "I love you, bitch, so much!"

Of course, when a foreigner comes up against this total linguistic chaos where words elbow in front of each other like winos in Great Digging lining up to buy apple vermouth (the cheapest liquor available in the old Soviet Union), despair sets in. But I do know one American who mastered real Russian flawlessly in a mere two days. I met this phenomenal linguist in 1979, five days after I arrived in the U.S. His name was Rabbi Bernstein and he was the head of a Jewish organization where I, a freshly minted émigré, went to interview for a job editing Jewish religious books in Russian, which paid a whopping $150 a week.

When I arrived, a tall man of fifty rose to greet me. He was wearing a yarmulke, a dark suit, and on his shoulders was a sprinkling of dandruff flakes. His nose was large and swollen from a cold.

"Good moRninG," I said, painstakingly enunciating all the letters in this phrase, including the *r* and the final *g*. (I had spent all of the previous day cramming and practicing polite English phrases of salutation.)

"*Yobaniy v rote!*" (Fucked in the mouth!) the rabbi said to me with a smile.

I decided that I had misheard him, and that probably he had said some polite phrase in English that I didn't know. So I came out with my next memorized phrase:

"How aRe you siR?"

"*Ne pizdi, paskuda yobaniy!*" said the rabbi, his smile growing broader. "*Kolis, padla!*" (Don't fuck me, you fuckin' shit! Come clean, you dick!)

At this point I understood that the rabbi's Russian was far better than my English. In any case, with these words in his vocabulary, he would never have any trouble in Russia. In fact, using these phrases he would be able to get anything he needed in Russia without ever standing in line, be it a train ticket or tickets to the theatre, a prescription at a pharmacy, or a job as a bartender. Why, with what he knew, the speaker of the Russian parliament would even yield him the podium without a whimper of protest. But where could a rabbi on

Fifth Avenue in New York have learned this Russian, which was so close to what the natives speak?

It turned out that the previous summer Rabbi Bernstein had made a tourist trip to Kiev. As soon as he landed and got off the plane, he had immediately taken a taxi to Babi Yar, the site where the Germans shot two hundred thousand Jews during World War II. Here the rabbi spread out a small prayer rug, knelt down, and began to recite the Kaddish, the Jewish prayer for the dead. Within ten minutes, KGB officers were at the cemetery. They flung themselves on the rabbi, twisted his arms behind his back, tossed him into a car, and bore him off to a basement room at the KGB, where for two days they beat and cursed him, demanding that he confess to being an American spy. During the two days they broke a finger on his right hand and he learned the real Russian that people actually speak—enough of it to communicate with any Russian from the president to a bunch of drunks standing in line at a liquor store.

I don't insist that everyone who plans to go to Russia take a crash course with teachers like *this*. That would be a bit extreme. But the question is, what is the minimum vocabulary someone needs to carry on a real conversation with Russians? I read somewhere that the English compiled a dictionary for foreign mercenaries in the British army containing two thousand words. So it seems that in a country whose language contains more than six hundred thousand words, it's possible to become a general with a knowledge of only two thousand. And since the largest Russian dictionary contains two hundred thousand, you can figure out for yourself that to serve in the Russian army requires only about seven hundred words. But even that is a monstrous exaggeration, and as a former Russian soldier I can assure you of this!

The famous twentieth-century Russian writers Ilya Ilf and Evgeny Petrov developed a dictionary back in the thirties that allows the user to get by in Russian in absolutely all situations—

and this dictionary contains a grand total of thirty words! In the second chapter of this book, we will go through it word by word.

What else do you need to know about this book to learn to speak real Russian quickly, easily, and to get an idea of how Russians really live? We don't have the space here to provide an encyclopedic guide to Russia, but I can guarantee that you will acquire one hundred times more knowledge than a Berlitz language course would give you. And this conviction also comes from my own personal experience.

In 1983 I signed a contract with Universal Studios in Hollywood for a screen version of my novel *Red Square*, which had become an international bestseller that year.

The producer invited me to Hollywood, sent a first-class ticket, and told me I would be staying at the Sheraton. I decided that this was my big break and that henceforth I would be fraternizing exclusively with Hollywood stars. To prepare myself, I went to Berlitz, which bills itself as "the world's best language school," and shelled out five hundred dollars for ten lessons. Even now that is no small change, and back then, it was big bucks. My teacher turned out to be a young Greek Marxist who spent all ten lessons using highbrow *New York Times*–style English to explain to me, an émigré from the USSR, why communism had it hands down over capitalism. I flew off to L.A. after the tenth lesson, crammed with elementary knowledge of English and a peculiar new perspective on the flaws of American society.

At the airport I was greeted by a well-dressed gentleman holding a sign that said MR. TOPOL. I shook his hand and embraced him in the hearty Russian fashion, like Brezhnev embracing Carter. He wanted to carry my suitcase, but I wouldn't give it to him. He led me to a black limo twenty meters long that looked like an SS-20 missile and opened the rear door for me. But in Russia, where there is "no exploitation of one human by another and all people are equal," no one ever sits in the back seat of a car, not even in a taxi. So I insisted on riding in the front seat next to him. As we drove to the hotel, I began discussing with him in my newly acquired highbrow English who he was planning to cast in the main role, Jack Nicholson or Robert Redford? After about ten minutes had passed, he realized that I had taken him for a producer, and in Spanglish he explained that he was a driver from a limo service.

I was vexed that I had spent five hundred bucks and then made such a hash of things. What I needed was a slim guide with instructions on how to handle common, everyday situations. So, as I worked on this book, I vowed that my readers would not find themselves in a similar bind! The result was

Dermo!—which will serve as your guide to the way real Russians live, communicate, and socialize every day. You should keep in mind that in Russia, unlike in other European countries, practically no one speaks English, and foreigners who don't speak Russian are constantly being duped: (*obmanut', nadut', ob'egorit', natyanut', sdelat', upotrebit', obut', prilozhit'*, etc., which in English mean: deceive, cheat, bamboozle, entrap, con, bilk, ensnare, do a number on, take for a ride, and so on) at every turn. You can see that there are enough terms in Russian meaning "to screw someone," to really take you for a ride no matter what the time or place.

And so, dear reader and student, onward and upward! The great and mighty Russian language, **мать его в три креста**! (remember: *mat' yevo v tri kresta!* that is, motherfucker and three crosses too!) awaits you on every page of this book. You can expect to learn at least two hundred **ёбаных** (*yobanich*, fucking) words of this language!

1
The Most Important Word in the Russian Language

I don't know how it is in other languages, but in Russia the operative word when it comes to cursing is *tier*, as in a three-tier or triple-decker curse, which consists of three levels of different curses stacked one on top of the other. (For example, **хуем пизданутыий мудак**, *huyem pizdanuty mudak*, jerk-off fucked by a prick.) When someone lets loose with a triple-decker curse, bystanders often remark, **обложил трехэтажным матом** (*oblozhil trekhetazhnim matom*—he lobbed him a triple-decker curse), and when the weapon of choice is a seven-tier curse, they are likely to say, **покрыл семиэтажным матом** (*pokryl semietazhnym matom*—he smashed him with a seven-storey curse). Can you feel the difference between *lob* and *smash*? (In Russian, **обложить** (*oblozhit'*) vs. **покрыть** (*pokryt'*), literally, *surround* vs. *bury*.)

The word **мат** (*mat*), Russian for *cursing*, is derived from the word for *mother* **мать** (pronounced *mat'*), and it is the root of all Russian swearing, which should be mastered by foreigners even before they learn to say *spasibo* (thank you) and *vodka*. Yes, oh yes, **мать** is truly a great word in Russian culture. It is a magical password to comradeship with strangers. It is enough for you to utter the phrase **твою мать!** *(tvoyu mat'!)* in the sense of *fuck your mother!* correctly and with confidence to be accepted as an intimate and a native in any group of Russians.

To teach you how to pronounce this correctly, I must introduce you to one linguistic oddity. The Russian alphabet contains a symbol which in and of itself has no sound, but which affects the pronunciation of the letter immediately preceding it. I am speaking of the **ь**, the soft sign. And so we have the soft **т** in the word **мать** *(mat')*, meaning *mother*, and in the word with the solitary **т**, without the soft sign, we have **мат** *(mat)*, signifying what in English are known as four-letter words (although in Russian they usually have more than four letters). So let us agree that wherever correct Russian pronunciation requires it, in the English transcription we will soften hard English consonants with the apostrophe in place of the Russian soft sign, as linguists do when transcribing words from the Cyrillic letters used in Russian into the Roman alphabet used in English. So instead of **мат** *(mat)* we have **мать** *(mat')*, instead of **вон!** *(von!)* (get out!) we have **вонь** *(von')* (stench), instead of **кон** *(kon)* (kitty—as in a poker game, not a cat) we have **конь** *(kon')* (horse).

Please note that in expressions where **мать** *(mat')* appears without the word "fuck," "fuck" is always implied. Although the literal translations of some of these phrases may not seem to make a whole lot of sense, they are all variants on a single theme, expressing varying degrees of intensity. All these phrases are based on the phrase **ёб твою мать** *(yob tvoyu mat')*, which means *motherfucker*, or literally, *I fucked your mother*. And so without further ado, here are two dozen of those four-letter words and profane phrases—**матерные выражения** *(maternye vyrazheniya)*—to start you out, given in ascending order, culminating with the very foulest. They will open any door and any heart in Russia.

2

Dermo!

Russian		
Cyrillic	**Transcription**	**Translation**
мать-перемать!	*mat'-peremat'!*	your mother twice over!
вашу мать!	*vashu mat'!*	your mother! (plural or formal)
твою мать!	*tvoyu mat'!*	your mother (sing. or informal)
мать твою растак!	*mat' tvoyu rastak!*	your mother like this and like that!
мать вашу так!	*mat' vashu tak!*	your mother like this!
мать вашу растуды!	*mat' vashu rastudy!*	your mother up, down, and all around!
мать их через семь гробов!	*mat' ikh cherez sem' grobov!*	their mother and seven coffins too!
так твою мать!	*tak tvoyu mat'!*	singular of *mat' vashu tak!* (above)
мать твою перемать!	*mat' tvoyu peremat'!*	variant of *mat'-peremat'* (above)
едри твою мать!	*edri tvoyu mat'!*	screw/frig your mother [somewhat gentler than ёб твою мать]
етти твою мать!	*etti tvoyu mat'!*	same as above
еби твою мать!	*ebi tvoyu mat'!*	fuck your mother! (imperative form)

Ёб твою мать!	*Yob tvoyu mat'!*	I fucked your mother!
мать твою за ногу!	*mat' tvoyu za nogu!*	your mother by the leg!
мать твою в три креста!	*mat' tvoyu v tri kresta!*	your mother and three crosses too!
еби твою бога душу мать!	*ebi tvoyu boga dushu mat'!*	fuck your mother, soul of God!
мать твою через семь ворот с присвистом!	*mat' tvoyu cherez sem' vorot s prisvistom!*	your mother through seven gates while whistling!
мать твою в гроб!	*mat' tvoyu v grob!*	your mother in her coffin!
Иди к чертовой матери!	*Idi k chertovoy materi!*	Go to the devil's mother!
Иди к ёбаной матери!	*Idi k yobani materi!*	Go to [your] fucking mother!

From the words **мать** and **мат** we get the words **материться** (*materit'sya*), **матюгаться** (*matyugat'sya*), and **матюкаться** (*matyukat'sya*), all meaning to express oneself using four-letter words, or to curse using dirty words, and also we get the words **матюг** or **матюк** that serve as components in certain expletive phrases.

Keep in mind that when used generally and addressed to no one in particular, these expressions are fairly inoffensive, but when they are addressed to a particular person, they immediately become deadly insults. In the Caucasus Mountains on

Russia's southwestern frontier, where passions run high and many people still live their lives according to ancient codes of honor and vengeance, you can end up paying with your life if you use the expression ёб твою мать! *(yob tvoyu mat'!)* with reference to a specific person (as opposed, we repeat, to addressing such remarks generally, to no one in particular).

Interestingly, one Russian dictionary published during the Soviet period asserts that the concept of swearing using the word мать is so vulgar that "there is no way that it could have originated in a Slavic environment," but must have entered the Russian language during the Tartar-Mongol invasion in the Middle Ages. If this is in fact the case, then it must be noted that the concept has, nonetheless, made itself quite at home in the Russian language and is common currency among all Russians. This is confirmed by Russian folklore, which has given us an entire poem on this subject:

> Есть русское слово такое,
> Дороже его не сыскать.
> Оно хоть и очень простое,
> Но русское, ёб твою матв!
> Возьмем, например, мужичонку,
> Он выехал рано пахать
> И крикнул своей лошаденке:
> "Ну, трогай же, ёб твоюмать!"
> Вот пьяный лежит под забором.
> Проснулся и начал рыдать:
> "Неужто помру тут с позором?
> О, Господи, ёб твою мать!"

> *Est' russkoye slovo takoye,*
> *Dorozhe evo ne syskat'.*
> *Ono khot' i ochen' prostoye,*
> *No russkoye, yob tvoyu mat'!*
> *Voz'myom, naprimer, muzhichonku,*

Dermo!

On vyekhal rano pakhat',
I kriknul svoyey loshadyonke,
"Nu, trogay zhe, yobe tvoyu mat'!"
Vot p'yaniy lezhit pod zaborom.
Prosnulsya i nachal rydat':
"Neuzhto pomru tut s pozorom?
O, Gospodi, yob tvoyu mat'!"

There is a certain Russian word,
Like nothing you have ever heard.
I'll be frank: Classy it's not;
Here's how it sounds: yob tvoyu mat'.

A farmer goes out to his field, let's say,
And starts to plow at the break of day.
He says to his horse, who won't budge from the spot:
"Get yer ass in gear, yob tvoyu mat'."

Or a drunk is sprawled on the ground
He moans and mutters as he comes around,
"Will I croak like a bum in this vacant lot?
Oh, good lord, yob tvoyu mat'."

And so on and so forth. This fine exclamation can be used in any situation that may arise in everyday life, as too can its abbreviated version—**ебёна мать** (*ebyona mat'*—fucking or frigging mother, also freely translated as "I'll be damned"). And we have another poem about this phrase, no less wonderful than the previous one:

Ебёна мать для русского народа
Как хлеб, как соль, как воздух и вода . . .
Но не затем, чтобы ругать,
А для того, чтобы сказать:
Ебёна мать!
Вот, например, такси позвать:

7

"Ну, поезжай быстрей, ебёна мать!"
Иль девушке любимой рассказать:
"Какая ты красивая, ебёна мать!"

Ebyona mat' dlya russkovo naroda
Kak khleb, kak sol', kak vozdukh i voda . . .
No ne zatem, shtoby rugat',
A dlya tovo, shtoby skazat':

Ebyona mat'!
Vot, naprimer, taksi pozvat':
"Nu, poezhay bystreye, ebyona mat'!"
Il' devushke lyubimoy rasskazat':
"Kakaya ty krasivaya, ebyona mat'!"

Ebyona mat', ebyona mat'
Now there's an expression that really says a lot!
It can blow cold, it can blow hot,
Is there any shade of meaning that this phrase hasn't got?

Clearer than water, purer than air,
Russians will insert these words anywhere,
They utter them not only when they swear,
A dialogue without them is really quite rare,
Ebyona mat', say it if you dare!

Ebyona mat', tossed off as if by chance,
Will inject some heat into a languishing romance,
Or make a sluggish cabby get the lead out of his pants,
There's not a thing that it won't enhance!
So squeeze your eyes shut and say *ebyona mat'*,
It'll make things better, more likely than not!

As you can see, Russian folklore serves as confirmation of that golden rule, that crucial secret of live Russian speech of which I wrote in the introduction.

And one last note before we set off to pay a visit to a Russian

Dermo!

home or join a bunch of Russians just sitting around talking. Of course this little book is not enough to elevate your knowledge of Russian to its pinnacle—the seventh tier—but you will probably make it to the third tier. And that is just as high as you need to go right now, as it is on precisely the third floor of the Kremlin that the president of Russia has his office.

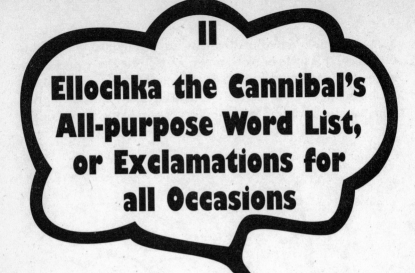

II

Ellochka the Cannibal's All-purpose Word List, or Exclamations for all Occasions

The novel *The Twelve Chairs*, by Ilya Ilf and Evgeny Petrov, is the story of two men who travel around Russia in search of an antique set of twelve dining room chairs, one of which has jewels hidden in it worth a million dollars. But the book became famous in Russia not just for the ingenious twists and turns of the plot, but for its hilarious humor. The book became more popular than the works of Chekhov, Gorky, and Tolstoy put together, and soon nearly everyone in the country was talking in quotations from it. The characters were as real to Russians as Batman is to Americans, Pickwick is to the English, or Inspector Maigret is to the French. One of these characters was Ellochka the Cannibal. This fine Muscovite lady vied with the New York millionairess Lady Vanderbilt for the title of "most glamorous." But instead of a mink coat, Ellochka wore a rabbit-fur dyed to look like mink (as her husband's earnings were quite modest), and rather than mining all the riches of the great and mighty Russian language, she got around relying almost exclusively on the following phrases and interjections:

Dermo!

1. **Хамите** *(Hameetye)* You're being rude.

2. **Хо-хо!** *(Ho-ho!)* Depending on the circumstances, this may express irony, amazement, ecstasy, hatred, joy, contempt, or satisfaction.

3. **Знаменито** *(Znamenito)* literally means *famous*, used as slang to mean cool, nifty.

4. **Мрачный** *(Mrachniy)* gloomy, grumpy. Can be used to describe anything at all. For example: "That grumpy guy Peter just got here," "gloomy weather," "gloomy situation," "grumpy cat."

5. **Мрак** *(Mrak)* literally, *gloom*, *bleakness*, used to mean, "how awful."

6. **Жуть** *(Zhut')* / **Жуткнй** *(Zhutkiy)* literally, *horrible* or *scary;* used as slang to mean something awesome. For example, if you meet someone you like, it's: "an awesome meeting."

7. **Парниша** *(Parnisha)* kiddo, buddy boy. Applied to all male acquaintances, regardless of age or social status.

8. **Не учите меня жить.** *(Ne uchitye menya zhit'.)* Don't teach me how to live, i.e., don't tell me what to do.

9. **Как ребенка** *(Kak rebyonka)* like a child. An intensifier, used like English "like a mug [in the sense of a "loser"]." **Я его бью как ребенка** *(I beat him like a child)* refers to a game of cards. **Я его срезала как ребенка** *(I cut him down to size like a child)* means "I put him in his place."

10. **Кр-р-расота!** *(Kr-r-rasota!)* Be-e-yoo-tiful!

11. **Толстый и красивый** *(Tolstiy and krasiviy)* Fat and pretty. Applied to inanimate as well as animate objects.

12. **Поедем на извозчике.** *(Poedem na izvozchike.)* Let's go in a hired carriage. Said to her husband.

13. **Поедем в таксо.** *(Poedem v takso.)* Let's go in a taxi. To male acquaintances.

14. **У вас вся спина белая.** *(U vas vsya spina belaya.)* Your back has white stuff all over it. (Joke.)

15. **Подумаешь.** *(Podumaesh'.)* Big deal.

11

16. **Уля** *('Ulya)* An affectionate diminutive put on the end of a name. For example: Misha = Mishulya. Sasha = Sashulya.

17. **Ого!** *(Ogo!)* Irony, amazement, ecstasy, hatred, joy, contempt, and satisfaction.

In the 1930s this lexicon and Ellochka the Cannibal herself became stock concepts and part of Russian culture. But as another classic Russian author, Maxim Gorky, said, "the Russian language is inexhaustibly rich and grows ever richer with stunning speed."

Recently, the Russian language has increased its assets so enormously that it has given rise to a new lexicon called **новоречь** *(novorech')*—new Russian language or "new-speak." And the main feature of all the new words now enriching the language of Tolstoy, Turgenev, and Chekhov is their vulgarity, and—not to put too fine a point on it—their jail-house origins. There is a simple explanation for this phenomenon: During the Soviet regime the Communists kept no fewer than twenty million people in prisons and labor camps, most of whom were men, many between the ages of fifteen and twenty. And now, in the 1990s, when the puritanical censorship in place under the Communists has come tumbling down along with the Soviet regime itself, all the camp folklore—the slang the criminals used, their underworld lingo, and songs—have surged onto the pages of newspapers and books, into pop music performances, and onto the radio and television airwaves. This lingo *is* today's Russian new-speak, and it is so widely used that even anchors on the national news shows use words that are essentially underworld terms without a hint of embarrassment. Terms such as **разборка** *(razborka)*, which used to mean violent score-settling in the underworld now refers to score-settling among politicians; **тусовка** *(tusovka)*, which used to mean a gathering of criminals, now means any gathering, get-together, or group of people hanging out, and so on. And as for the country's new leaders and parliamentarians, it goes without saying that almost all of them are former Communist functionaries who even in the old days conversed among themselves in a language consisting exclusively of four-letter words.

And so here are some additions to the lexicon of Ellochka the Cannibal, words and phrases that are apt, practical, and suited to any and all situations in today's Russia.

не слабо! *(ne slabo!)* Literally, *not weak!* in the sense of **клево** *(klyovo*—nifty), **здорово** *(zdorovo*—great) and **хорошо** *(khorosho*—cool). (This replaces the words **жуть** *(zhut')* and **красота** *(krasota)* in the lexicon of Ellochka the Cannibal.)

однако! *(odnako!)* Literally, *however*, used to express amazement, respect, or confusion, like the English phrase, "Well, how about that?"

пиздец! *(pizdets!)* Literally, *cunt, vagina*, used to express both delight and upset at a fiasco, the end of the world, etc. For example: **Вчера видел бабу – ну, пиздец! Богиня!** *(Vchera videl babu – nu, pizdets! boginya!* English: Yesterday I saw this chick, she was a fucking goddess!) Or, to the contrary: **Ну, уродина – пиздец!** *(Nu, urodina – pizdets!* What a fucking dog!) Or: **Мне полный пиздец – только что проиграл на бирже десять миллионов!** *(Mnye polny pizdets – tol'ko shto proigral na birzhe desyat millionov!* I'm screwed—I just lost ten million on the stock market! What a drag.)

ё-моё! *(yo-moyo!)* A softer version of **ёб твою мать** *(yob tvoyu mat')*, like saying *sugar* instead of *shit*. This expression is used to express amazement, disappointment, and annoyance as are the expressions **ёлки-палки!** *(yolki-palki*—for crying out loud), **японский бог!** *(yaponskiy bog!*, literally, *Japanese god*, translatable as *Ye gads!)*, **японский городовой!** *(yaponskiy gorodovoy!* literally, *Japanese*

policeman! A comparable English phrase would be *Jeez Louise!* or *Gee whiz!*) and **ёксель-моксель!** (*yoksel'-moksel'!* which means something like *Jeepers creepers! Gee willikers!* or *Wow!*). These expressions are used in moments of surprise, distress, sadness, etc.

офигеть можно! or охуеть можно! (*ofiget' mozhno* or *ohuyet' mozhno*)—expressions of delight, ecstasy. From the word хуй (*huy*), meaning prick or dick. For example: Сегодня день – офигеть можно: солнце светит, птички поют! Ну, полный пиздец! (*Sevodnya den' – ofiget' mozhno: solntse svetit, ptichki poyut! Nu, pol'niy pizdetz!* What a fucking beautiful day!—the sun is shining, the birds are singing. It's enough to make you shit!)

15

бля! (*blya!*) or more strongly, **бляха-муха!** (*blyakha-mukha!*)—from the word **блядь** (*blyad'*), meaning ~~whore~~ (not to be taken literally in this particular expression). These express surprise, delight, distress, vexation. For example: **У неё сиськи – бляха-муха! – по пуду каждая!** (*U neyo sis'ki – blyakha-mukha! – po pudu kazhdaya!* Did you see the knockers on that babe? Shee-it! They were the size of melons!*) Or: **Всё, бляха-муха, устала плясать! Не могу и рукой шевельнуть!** (*Vsyo, blyakha-mukha, ustala plyasat'! Ne mogu i rukoy shevel'nut'!* Holy shit, I'm pooped, I can't dance another step.)

блин! (*blin!*) Same as *blya*, but it applies to men.

Ну ты даёшь! (*Nu ty dayosh'!*) Well, look at you! or, What will you think of next! or, Well, how about that! said to someone who has done something surprising or unexpected.

хана! (*hana!*) or **хана дело!** (*hana delo!*) or **труба дело!** (*truba delo!*) and also **кранты!** (*kranty!*) Signifies a fiasco, an unsuccessful finish, or a loss. What a flop! What a washout! The game is up! It's curtains for us, fellows.

заебись! (*zayebis'!*) Used to express any emotion from ecstasy to despair. For example: **Ну, у тебя шляпка – заебись!** *Nu u tebya shlyapka – zayebis'!*—That hat is hot shit! Really slick! Or: **Да заебись ты в жопу со своей шляпой! Отстань от меня!** *Da zayebis' ty v zhopu so svoyay shlyapkoy! Otstan' ot menya!* Fuck off with your fucking hat! Leave me alone!

халява (*halyava*) Freebie. Any party, reception, or function where there is free food.

крыша (*krysha*) Literally, *roof*, used to mean *protector*, *underworld patron*, *cover*, *backer*, i.e., the person or organization who protects a businessperson from racketeers or the police.

крыша поехала *(krysha poekhala)* Literally, *his roof flew off,* used to mean *he went crazy,* or to describe someone who does something inexplicably strange. For example: **Они ему такое сказали, что он – всё, свихнулся, у него крыша поехала!** (*Oni emu takoye skazali, shto on – vsyo, svikhnulsya, u nevo krysha poekhala!* They told him something so amazing/outrageous that he flipped, he went bonkers!) Or: **У тебя что – крыша поехала? Ты с ума сошел?** (*U tebya shto – krysha poekhala? Ty s uma soshel?* What's wrong with you—are you off your rocker? Have you lost your mind?)

бабки *(babki)* Dough, as in money.

Ты меня уважаешь? *(Ty menya uvazhaesh?)* Do you respect me? A question invariably asked by Russians after they have polished off their first liter of vodka. When you hear this question, you know it's time to call a halt to the drinking spree, because your Russian friend is already plastered.

Ну ты хорош! *(Nu ty khorosh!)* Literally, *Well, you're a fine one!* used to mean *You're feeling no pain,* or *You're pretty far gone,* used to signify an advanced stage of drunkenness and the accompanying condemnation, amazement and/or censure by the drunk's companions. For example: **Выпил пол-литра и был хорош!** (*Vypil pol-litra i byl khorosh!* He knocked back half a liter and was feeling no pain.)

по определению *(po opredeleniyu)* By definition. Used to intensify or accentuate. For example: **Он идиот по определению!** (*On idiot po opredeleniyu!*—He is an idiot by definition!) Or: **Она проститутка по определению!** (*Ona prostitutka po opredeleniyu!*—She is the very definition of a prostitute!)

челнок *(chelnok)* Peddler, a small wholesale dealer, often a woman, who shuttles back and forth across borders, bringing in merchandise in her own luggage.

заморочки *(zamorochki)* Monkey business, tricks, swindles, minor scams, also known as **примочки** *(primochki)*.

левак *(levak)* A car owner who works illegally or unofficially as a taxi driver, from the word **лево** *(levo)* meaning *left side*, indicating that the driver is operating on the side or under the table.

Among other notable emendations to Ellochka the Cannibal's vocabulary list, we draw your attention to the fact that these days instead of saying *let's go in a hired carriage*, women now say to their husbands, *let's take the subway*, and instead of *fat and pretty*, the term in use now is **крутой!** *(krutoy!)*, which means *tough!* or *cool!* Nonetheless, the use of any expression at all from Ellochka the Cannibal's vocabulary list will not only reveal your profound knowledge of Russian speech as spoken by real people, but will also demonstrate your lofty literary erudition.

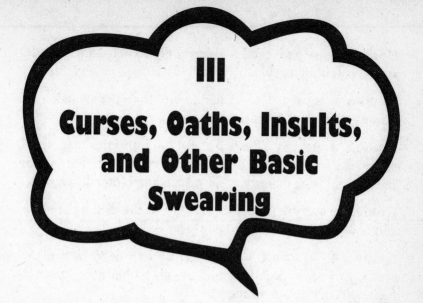

III
Curses, Oaths, Insults, and Other Basic Swearing

In business and courtship it is extremely important to understand where your Russian partners (or heartthrobs) are telling you to go. (As in "you know where you should go?" "go to hell!" and so on.)

Here are the standard destinations to which Russians generally send others, at least verbally. We present them in ascending order of distance and depth.

Пошел к дьяволу! *(Poshol k d'yavolu!)* Go to the devil! This destination is quite nearby and not insulting.

Пошел ты! *(Poshol ty!)* same as *poshol k d'yavolu!*

Пошел ты куда подальше! *(Poshol ty kuda podal'she!)* Get outta here! or Get away from here!

Пошел ты знаешь куда?! *(Poshol ty znaesh' kuda?!)* You know where you should go?!

These last three are not distant and not insulting.

Пошел к черту *(Poshol k chortu)* Go to hell—a little ruder and a bit farther away.

Пошел в жопу *(Poshol v zhopu)* Go (in)to the ass *(whose* ass is not specified). This is rude, but not terribly so.

Пошел в пизду *(Poshol v pizdu)* Go (in)to the cunt (again, not stated whose). This is not simply rude, now, but getting serious, and most important, the destination is literally *deep*.

Пошел на хуй *(Poshol na hui)* Go to the dick. (Very rude and unaesthetic.)

Пошел к ёбаной матери *(Poshol k yobaniy materi)* Literally, *go to your fucked mother*, or, go to hell, you motherfucker. (A deliberate insult.)

Будь ты проклят / проклята! *(Bud' ty proklyat / proklyata!)* (masculine/feminine) May you be cursed! or Damn you!

Чтоб ты сдох / сдохла! *(Shtob ty sdokh!)* (masc.) *sdokhla!* (fem.) May you drop dead! Or simply, drop dead!

Чтоб ты сгорел / сгорела! *(Shtob ty sgorel!)* (masc.) *sgorela!* (fem.) May you burn!

Чтоб тебя нечистая сила забрала! *(Shtob tebya nechistaya sila zabrala!)* May dark [impure] forces carry you away!

В гробу я тебя видал! *(V grobu ya tebya vidal!)* May I see you in your coffin! or alternatively, I saw you in your coffin! The latter means, I dreamed that I saw you in your coffin and may this dream come true!

Чтоб ты меня видел одним глазом и я тебя одноногим! *(Shtob ty menya videl odnim glazom, i ya tebya* *odnonogim!)* May you see me with one eye, and I see you with one leg! (joke)

Чтоб ты пропал! *(Shtob ty propal!)* May you disappear! (hardly serious)

Чтоб ты провалился! *(Shtob ty provalilsya!)* May the earth swallow you up! (half-serious)

Гори ты синим пламенем! *(Gori ty sinim plamenem)* May you burn in a dark blue flame. (almost serious)

It's curious that in not one of these curses, even in the joking ones, is there a single **ь**, soft sign. Softness would be out of place here.

Oaths

Back in the year 922, Akhmed Ibn Falan, the first ambassador to Russia from the caliph of Persia, noted that "within their country the people of Rus have little trust for each other. They always carry a sword, and treachery is common among them. If one of them manages to acquire even a small amount of property, his own brother or friend immediately starts to envy him and tries to kill or rob him. Even when they go to answer the call of nature they go not alone but accompanied by two or three comrades and with their swords which they place near themselves."

Perhaps because of this tendency, Russians have accumulated an enormous number of oaths to preserve themselves from their own perfidy and betrayal. A simple **даю слово!** (*dayu slovo*—I give you my word!) is never enough. At every turn one hears demands that at times may seem excessive, yet using them is the only way the speaker can guarantee the truth of his words and promises: For example, **забожись!** (*zabozhis'*—swear!) or **поклянись!** (*poklyanis'*—take an oath!) or **скажи: сука буду!** (*skazhi, suka budu*—Say: I'll be a bitch if . . . ! i.e., if I don't keep my word). Like the English "Cross my heart, hope to die/stick a needle in my eye."

Here are some oaths and the words that serve to make these oaths binding:

Ей богу! (*Yei bogu*) By God! (A minor little oath, not serious, practically an interjection.)

Клянусь богом! (*Klyanus' bogom!*) I swear by God! (More often than not, means that the person is lying.)

Даю слово! (*Dayu slovo*) I give you my word! (Not to be relied upon.)

Даю вам честное слово! (*Dayu vam chestnoye slovo!*) I give you my word of honor! (Very unreliable.)

Гад буду! (*Gad budu!*) I'll be a skunk/louse! Meaning, I'll be a louse if I don't keep my word, or, I'll be a louse if this isn't true. Even so, you are not expected to believe.

Сука буду! (*Suka budu!*) I'll be a bitch! (The same, only stronger.)

Падла буду! (*Padla budu!*) I'll be scum! (Even stronger, but still not worth believing.)

Чтоб я сдох / сдохла! (*Shtob ya sdokh!*) (masc.) or *shtob ya sdokhla!* (fem.) May I drop dead! [if I do not keep my word]. (Very strong, but still not to be relied on.)

Век свободы не видать! (*Vek svobodi ne vidat'!*) May I not see freedom for an eon! or **Век воли не видать!** (*Vek voli ne vidat'!*) May I not be at liberty for an eon! (These phrases arose in the criminal world among prisoners and are used half-jokingly in everyday life.)

Клянусь матерью! (детьми, сыном, дочкой) (*Klyanus' materyu! [det'mi, synom, dochkoy]*) I swear by my mother! or by my children, by my son, by my daughter. These are getting serious, especially if the whole phrase is used: **Клянусь здоровьем своих детей!** (*Klyanus' zdorov'em svoikh detay!*) I swear by my children's health! And said this way it's even better: **Клянусь жизнью своих детей!** (*Klyanus' zhizn'yu svoikh detay!*) I swear by my children's lives!

Клянусь матери могилой! (*Klyanus' materi mogiloy!*) I swear by my mother's grave! (A very serious oath to someone from the Caucasus.)

Гореть мне в аду синим пламенем! *(Goret' mne v adu sinim plamenem!)* May I burn in hell in a dark blue flame! (Completely unserious.)

Before conversion to Christianity a mere thousand years ago, Russians were pagans, and they have retained pagan beliefs and superstitions to this day. Perhaps this is the reason they do not take seriously oaths that mention the name of God and violate them without a second thought. They are afraid, however, to violate an oath taken on their children's health or lives and believe that only the lowest of the low would be capable of such a thing. So when you sign a contract with a Russian, it's not a bad idea to give it extra force with the words **Клянусь здоровьем своих детей** (*Klyanus' zdorov'em svoikh detey*—I swear by my children's health).

Keep in mind, though, that Russians take their favorite curses very seriously and don't appreciate hearing them made fun of.

Swearwords

Let's move on to swearwords. There are a fairly large number of them in Russian and one cannot know them all. Some say that there is no need to know them all—there is, after all, plenty of filth and foulness in the world without making a special effort to seek it out! This was the reasoning followed by a certain esteemed American politician when he learned that his daughter was taking a course in Russian four-letter words. The politician raised a huge ruckus over this, yelling about how our universities are spending the taxpayers' money on subjects that are worse than useless, harmful and so on. The uproar practically made its way all the way to Congress! But then someone explained the issue to him in terms he could grasp: He was told that if there were no linguists in the civil service with knowledge of Russian four-letter words, the government radio interception service would be totally useless, since Russian military pilots speak a patois that is three quarters four-letter words, and that the same is true of New Russian businessmen, and so on.

And so here are some verbs based on a few important roots; verbs that Russian pilots, businessmen, athletes, intellectuals, and politicians—and virtually everyone else—use all the time, verbs that you must know because without them you won't be able to do a thing in Russia.

	Transcription	Literal Translation	What It Really Means
ё бнуть	*yobnut'*	to fuck	to hit, to steal
ё бнуть по кумполу	*yobnut' po kumpolu*	to fuck in the head	to clobber in the head, to brain someone
ё бни его!	*yobni evo!*	fuck him!	clobber him, shoot him!
пиздануть	*pizdanut'*	cunt (*verb form*)	to whack, to steal
хуйнуть	*huynut'*	dick (*verb form*)	to whack, to steal
засветить	*zasvetit'*	to hit/ literally, to make someone see sparks/stars	to beat the living daylights out of someone
охуячить	*ohuyachit'*	dick (*verb*)	to hit
садануть	*sadanut'*	—	to bop someone
въебать	*v'ebat'*	to fuck	to hit, to sock someone
двинуть по рылу	*dvinut' po rylu*	to hit in the snout	to smack in the face, to punch in the nose

	Transcription	Literal Translation	What It Really Means
пырнуть	*pyrnut'*	—	to stab
наебать	*nayebat'*	to give someone a fucking	to hoodwink, to take for a ride
объебать	*ob'ebat'*	to fuck someone from all sides	to screw someone over
объегорить	*ob'egorit'*	—	to swindle
сделать	*sdelat'*	to do someone	to pull a fast one on someone, or to kill
отпиздить	*otpizdit'*	to cunt someone off	to beat someone up
припиздить	*pripizdit'*	to cunt someone in	to beat someone until they are barely left alive, to maul, to thrash
спиздить	*spizdit'*	to cunt something away from	to swipe

Insults

When you're in a foreign country and people call you various strange-sounding names, it never hurts to know what they mean. If nothing else, it's a way of learning about yourself from what other people think of you. And if you learn these words, you can then turn around and use them on people who don't know Russian and have some fun yourself!

Here is a brief selection of Russian insults, including those you are likely to hear most often in Russia:

Feminine	Masculine	Translation
дура (*dura*)	дурак (*durak*)	fool
идиотка (*idiotka*)	идиот (*idiot*)	idiot
кретинка (*kretinka*)	кретин (*kretin*)	cretin
остолопка (*ostolopka*)	остолоп (*ostolop*)	numbskull
мудачка (*mudachka*)	мудак (*mudak*)	dimwit, screw-up
мудила (*mudila*) (m. and f.)		nincompoop, fuck-up
гадина (*gadina*)	гад/гадина (*gad/gadina*)	louse, skunk, rat
грымза (*grymza*)		ugly rat
	подлец (*podlets*)	rascal
	козёл (*kozyol*)	goat
	козёл усратый (*kozyol usraty*)	shitty goat

Feminine	Masculine	Translation
	к о з ё л **ё б а н н ы й** *(kozyol yobanniy)*	fucked goat
п а д л а *(padla)*		base, despicable character
п а д а л ь *(padal')*		fallen woman; literally, *road kill* or *carrion* from **п а д а т ь** *(padat')*, meaning to fall
с в о л о ч ь *(svoloch')* (m. and f.)		bastard
ш к у р а *(shkura)*		harlot
	у б л ю д о к *(ublyudok)*	cur, mongrel, bastard
	н е д о н о с о к *(nedonosok)*	prematurely born (and presumably not all there intellectually or physically)
с у к а *(suka)*		bitch
с у ч а р а *(suchara)*		*real* bitch
	кобель, **кобель старый** *(kobel', kobel' stariy)*	male dog/mutt, old male dog
кобыла, кобыла **старая** *(kobyla, kobyla staraya)*		mare, nag/old nag

Feminine	Masculine	Translation
мразь *(mraz')* (m. and f.)		the dregs, bottom of the bucket
жертва аборта *(zhertva aborta)* (m. and f.)		abortion victim
тля *(tlya)*		plant louse
рыло *(rylo)* (m. and f.)		[pig] snout
мурло *(murlo)* (m. and f.)		ugly mug
шмягадявка *(shmyagadiavka)*		vermin
	прошмандовка *(proshmandovka)*	boy prostitute, hustler
подстилка *(podstilka)*		literally, *doormat*, a sexually loose woman
прохиндейка *(prokhindeyka)*	прохиндей *(prokhindey)*	flimflam artist
долдонка *(doldonka)*	долдон *(doldon)*	lout
дубина *(dubina)* (m. and f.)		blockhead
дубина стоеросовая *(dubina stoyerosovaya)* (m. and f.)		oaf

Feminine	Masculine	Translation
г о в н о *(govno)*	**г о в н ю к** *(govnyuk)*	shit, shithead (Lenin's favorite word)
ж о п а *(zhopa)*		ass
ж о п а с р у ч к о й *(zhopa s ruchkoy)*		literally, *an ass with a handle*, helpless, a basket case, clod
	р а з э д а к и й *(razyedakiy)*	euphemism for fucked-up; someone who is a mess
	р а з ъ е б а й *(razyebi)*	a fuckup, a screwup
р а з з я в а *(razzyava)*		airhead
р а с т е р ё х а *(rasteryokha)*		a flake
с в о л о т а *(svolota)*		first-class bastard
(с т а р а я) п е р е ч н и ц а *(staraya) perechnitsa*		(old) pepper mill
	(с т а р ы й) п е р д у н *(stariy) perdun*	(old) fart
у р о д и н а *(urodina)*		gargoyle
у р о д к а *(urodka)*	**в ы р о д о к** *(vyrodok)*	geek freak [congenitally deformed]

31

Feminine	Masculine	Translation
сикушка *(sikushka)*		child prostitute
	сифилитик *(sifilitik)*	syphilitic
	псих *(psikh)*	a nut case
	псих ненормальный *(psikh nenormalniy)*	a crazy nut
	сукин сын *(sukin syn)*	son of a bitch
стерва *(sterva)*	**стервец** *(stervets)*	harpy
негодяйка *(negodyai)*	**негодяй** *(negodyaika)*	reprobate
стерлядь *(sterlyad')*		virago
зануда *(zanuda)*		tedious creep
	хрен *(khren')*	literally, *horse-radish*, euphemism for **хуй** *(hui)*, meaning dick/prick/cock (because of similar sound)
	хрен моржовый *(khren morzhoviy)*	literally, *walrus dick*, jerk

Feminine	Masculine	Translation
	хер моржовый *(kher morzhoviy)*	same as above
хрычовка *(khrychovka)*	**хрыч** *(khrych)*	grouch
	старый хрыч *(stariy khrych)*	old grouch
чокнутая *(choknutaya)*	**чокнутый** *(choknutiy)*	crazy, off one's rocker
язва *(yazva)*		fishwife, literally, *ulcer*
	бздун *(bzdun)*	chicken (i.e., coward)
	балбес *(balbes)*	dunderhead
	бабник *(babnik)*	womanizer, skirt-chaser
бандитка *(banditka)*	**бандит** *(bandit)*	bandit, outlaw
беспутница *(besputnitsa)*	**беспутник** *(besputnik)*	libertine
блядина *(blyadina)*		big-time whore
	блядун *(blyadun)*	lecher
блядь полосатая *(blyad' polosataya)*		flaming whore (literally, *striped whore*)

Feminine	Masculine	Translation
последная блядь *(poslednaya blyad')*		as whorish as they come
	бугай *(bugay)*	fat, sleazy man with a taste for women
вертихвостка *(vertikhvostka)*		an ass-swinger, hussy
гондон *(gondon)*		rubber (condom)
дохлая задница *(dokhlaya zadnitsa)*		dead ass
дохлячка *(dokhlyachka)*		dead meat
дрянь *(dryan')*		piece of trash
драная кошка *(dranaya koshka)*		slattern
жаба *(zhaba)*		toad
жеребец *(zherebets)*		stud, brute (literally, *stallion*)
жук *(zhuk)*		beetle, sneaky person
жук навозный *(zhuk navozniy)*		manure beetle
жучок *(zhuchok)*		beetle (diminutive)

Dermo!

Feminine	Masculine	Translation
задница (*zadnitsa*)		rump, butt, rear end
старая задница (*staraya zadnitsa*)		old rump
пизда задрипанная (*pizda zadry-pannaya*)		cunt soiled with feces
задрыга (*zadryga*)		vapid, bedraggled woman

Feminine	Masculine	Translation
	очкарик *(ochkarik)*	four eyes
	интеллигент сраный *(intelligent sraniy')*	shitty intellectual, nerd
кастрат *(kastrat)*		castrated man
клизма (старая) *klizma (staraya)*		enema (old), douche bag
манда *(manda)*		cunt
мандавошка *(mandavoshka)*		Literally, cunt-louse, meaning pubic louse, crabs

If you learn even half of these words, you will feel right at home in Russia.

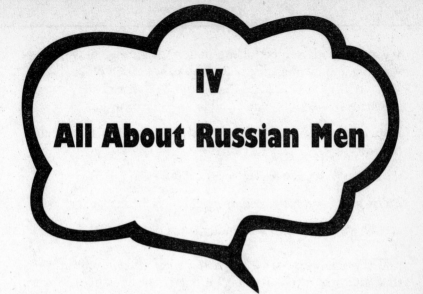

IV
All About Russian Men

Men in Russia fall into two categories, *men* and *not-men*—in other words, those who are "real men" and those who are "not men at all." When people say of someone **он настоящий мужчина** (*On nastoyaschiy muzhschina*—He is a real man), they are talking primarily not about his sexual prowess, but about the fact that he is true to his word, that he is a gentleman who knows how to conduct himself in polite society, and so on.

Then there are the categories *muzhik* and not-*muzhik*. The concept of **русский мужик** (*russkiy muzhik*) has negative connotations beyond Russia's borders, even indicating contempt, and usually signifies bad manners, rudeness, boorishness, barbarous behavior, and dissolute lewdness. But in Russia the word **мужик** has several meanings and precisely which one is intended in any given situation depends on the speaker's intonation.

мужик (with contemptuous intonation) A rude, uneducated person.

мужик (with respectful intonation) A strong, brave, hard-working and businesslike man, who is not afraid of hard work.

Various adjectives may be added for clarification:

верный мужик (*verniy muzhik*)—a true man (reliable, tested)

крепкий мужик (*krepkiy muzhik*)—a tough man

сильный мужик (*sil'niy muzhik*)—a strong man

мужлан (*muzhlan*)—a crude man, a boor, an oaf

If a woman says **мой мужик** (*moy muzhik*, my muzhik) this indicates pride in her husband's businesslike, serious, hardworking qualities.

крутой мужик (*krutoy muzhik*) Until recently, this was rendered in full as **мужик с крутым характером** (*muzhik s krutym kharakterom*, a muzhik with a tough personality) i.e., explosive, angry, unmanageable and high-handed. Now, though, in new-speak **крутой мужик** means a man who gets his business up and running quickly.

хозяин (*khozyain*) Master or boss. A very respectful term for a man—meaning real man, real boss, big guy, the person in charge.

дерьмо-мужик (*der'mo-muzhik*)—shit-man, i.e., worthless

нежный мужик (*nezhniy muzhik*)—a man who is tender

хороший мужик (*horoshiy muzhik*)—a good man

правильный мужик (*pravilniy muzhik*)—a man who is fair in his dealings

деловой мужик (*delovoy muzhik*)—a man who's doing serious business, not fooling around

дельный мужик (*del'niy muzhik*)—a man who knows what he's doing and does it right

нужный мужик (*nuzhniy muzhik*)—a man who is useful or valued in business

A Russian man's sexual prowess lies somewhere on a continuum between the words **чистый импотент** (*chistiy impotent*, a total impotent), **порожняк** (*porozhnyak*, an empty or hollow person), and **скопец** (*skopets*, a man who has been castrated), at one end of the spectrum, and **зверский ёбарь** (*zverskiy yobar'*, brutal fucker), at the other.

Here is a listing of everything between those extremes:

слабак (*slabak*)—a wimp

слабоёб (*slaboyob*)—a weak fuck

ништяк (*nishtyak*)—capable of satisfying, also a general term denoting approbation or a positive attitude toward something or someone

боец (*boyets*)—literally, *a fighting man*, a man capable of scaling sexual heights

ебака (*yebaka*)—someone who loves to fuck

настоящий мужик (*nastoyaschiy muzhik*)—a real muzhik, a man of sexual prowess

ёбарь (*yobar'*)—same as above

мужик что надо! (*muzhik shto nado!*)—a hell of a guy! (a great compliment)

мужик-заебись! (*muzhik-zayebis'!*)—a man who really gets it on! (This phrase signifies delight on the part of the speaker.)

злой ёбарь *(zloy yobar')* A nasty fucker, meaning a pitiless or merciless fucker, a sex-machine. There is even a little ditty about this type of man:

Пизда разъебана до сраки,
Какие злые есть ебаки!

Pizda raz'yobana do sraki,
Kakie zlye est' yebaki!

Nasty fuckers view seduction as a kind of sneak attack,
They will bang a girl clear through to her asshole and back,
When all she expected was a roll in the sack!

зверский ёбарь *(zverskiy yobar')* Brutal fucker. (The highest praise of someone's sexual abilities.)

убивец *(ubivets)* Literally, *killer*, signifies a man capable of fucking someone to death, and also describes a male organ—a "rod"—of monstrous, lethal dimensions.

V

A Bit About Russian Women

Like Rolls-Royces and the works of Botticelli, Russian women need no advertisement. In the Middle Ages many European monarchs fell in love with Russian princesses and offered them hand, heart, and throne. In our day this tradition has grown to the point where there is hardly a foreign bachelor who, after even a month in Russia, departs without a wife. This is because Russian women are amazingly beautiful and hardworking, as well as uniquely gentle, kind, and faithful to their husbands. Akhmed ibn Fadlan was the first but not the last traveller to ancient Rus who was struck by the beauty of Russian women. "I have never seen lovelier women, they are tall and slim like palm trees, and white of face and body," he wrote to his *padishah*. "Everyone who visited the country was struck by their loveliness and all were delighted by the fact that when her master died and the relatives cremated his body, a Russian girl would follow her beloved's body into the flames and burn with him."

The great and mighty Russian language has a word for every feature of the Russian woman's character and form.

красавица	*krasavitsa*	beauty, beautiful woman
красавица писанная	*krasavitsa pisannaya*	woman as pretty as a picture
краля	*kralya*	woman of regal beauty
пава	*pava* Literally, *peahen* [female peacock]	a woman of queenly carriage
дива	*diva*	ravishing as a fairy tale heroine
дева	*deva*	lass
девица	*devitsa*	virgin, a maiden
девушка	*devushka*	young maiden
барышня	*baryshnya*	nubile [marriageable] girl
целка	*tselka*	virgin, literally, *intact or whole*
старая дева	*staraya deva*	old maid
девица красная	*devitsa krasnaya*	bonnie lass
красотка	*krasotka*	a stunner
любушка	*lyubushka*	sweetie
голуба	*goluba*	dove [a pet name]
кукла	*kukla*	literally, *doll*, i.e., pretty girl
лапушка	*lapushka*	sweetie pie, literally, *little paw*
душка	*dushka*	sweet, sincere girl, sweetie

дорогая/ дроля	*dorogaya/drolya*	dear
милая	*milaya*	sweet girl
милаха	*milakha*	sweet darling girl (diminutive)
милка	*milka*	sweet darling girl (diminutive)
ненаглядная	*nenaglyadnaya*	beloved, literally, *a woman whom one never tires of gazing at; a sight for sore eyes*
любимая	*lyubimaya*	beloved
зазноба	*zaznoba*	lady love
тёлка	*tyolka*	babe, broad (a rude, casual way of referring to any woman, literally, *heifer*)
девка	*devka*	gal
девка не промах	*devka ne promakh*	a girl who doesn't miss a shot, a girl who is on the ball, ahead of the curve
давалка	*davalka*	a woman who puts out (from **дать**— *dat'*, meaning *to give*)
даваха	*davakha*	same as *davalka*

честная давалка	chestnaya davalka	good-time girl, literally, *honest giver*—a woman who is after sex, not for money, but for her own pleasure
дама	dama	a high-society woman, a woman who has some sexual experience
дамочка	damochka	a woman with a high opinion of herself, or social pretensions
баба	baba	a peasant wife, the wife, the old lady, broad (general term for a woman)
бабёнка	babyonka	a spunky young woman
бабище	babische	a tall woman
бабец	babets	a luscious babe, also someone who is built like a barn
станок-баба	stanok-baba	a woman who is really built or stacked
бой-баба	boi-baba	a feisty, shrewd woman, literally, *fighting woman*

конь-баба	kon'-baba	literally, *stallion woman*, also, **баба с йцами**— *baba s yitsami*, literally, *a woman with balls* (both terms mean an assertive woman, a woman who wears the pants)
дрянь	dryan'	a worthless woman, literally, *junk*
блядь	blyad'	whore, cheap prostitute, dissolute woman, slut
блядище	blyadische	a real whore [intensifier]
портовая блядь	portovaya blyad'	port or harbor whore
вокзальная блядь, гостиничная блядь	vokzal'naya blyad', gostinichnaya blyad'	train-station whore, hotel whore (depending on where she plies her trade)
шалава	shalava	tramp
курва	kurva	shrew, harridan
шельма	shel'ma	a loose woman who is a con artist to boot

плутовка	*plutovka*	a wily slut
чертовка	*chertovka*	a designing woman
шлюха	*shlyukha*	floozy, tart
валютная шлюха	*valyutnaya shlyukha*	hard-currency prostitute
валютная блядь	*valyutnaya blyad'*	hard-currency whore
шваль	*shval'*	trash
шалашовка	*shalashovka*	streetwalker, a homeless woman who turns tricks to survive
сука	*suka*	bitch
засранка	*zasranka*	literally, *a woman who shits on things*
подсирушка	*podsirushka*	dirty double-crosser
паскуда	*paskuda*	scum
проблядь	*problyad'*	super slut
проблядь-клейма негде ставить	*problyad'-kleima negde stavit'*	all-around whore
блядь ебучая	*blyad' ebuchaya*	a whore who is on the prowl or cruising, literally, fucking whore
мерзавка	*merzavka*	heel
гнида	*gnida*	nit [insect]

47

пиздорванка	*pizdorvanka*	bitch, fucker, whore, literally, *torn cunt*
хуесоска	*huesoska*	cocksucker, fellatrix
дешевка	*deshovka*	cheap whore, easy lay, trash
оторва	*otorva*	low-down good-for-nothing, ball-buster

(and so on—see chapter 3)

And although the second half of this list contains descriptions of the Russian women at odds with those of Akhmed ibn Fadlan and Ivan Turgenev, the author seconds the assessment of the ancient Persian, "Women fairer than Russian women I have never seen!"

Or maybe I just have bad luck with foreign women.

VI

Lovemaking, Russian Style

Recently, I got into an argument with my wife. It all started when I read her a quotation from Prosper Mérimée on the Russian language.

"The Russian language, insofar as I can make a judgment about it," said the eminent Frenchman, "is the richest of the European tongues and seems specially created to express the subtlest shades of meaning. Endowed with a wonderful compression of form combined with clarity, it can use one word to convey a thought for which another language would require an entire sentence."

My wife, who is Russian, sat wreathed in smiles as she listened to this. Then I read her a quote from Friedrich Engels:

"How beautiful is the Russian language! All the advantages of German without its dreadful crudeness." And immediately, without pausing, I said, "And now find me a Russian equivalent for the English expression *to make love*."

She thought long and hard. In Russian there really is not a single decent word to describe this activity. Even the words **любодейство** (*lyubodaystvo*) and **любодей** (*lyuboday*), which are direct calques based on the words *lovemaking* and *lovemaker* in Russian signify only decadence, lewdness, and licentiousness, and sound judgmental, differing from the Russian word for *adultery*, **прелюбодейство** *(prelyubodaystvo)*, by a mere syllable. Of course there are as many crude, vulgar, and unprintable words on this topic as anyone could ever wish for, but not a single one that can be used in polite company.

"It has to do with national traditions and national character—it isn't a reflection on the Russian language!" my wife said in an aggrieved tone. "Language expresses the national character, and not vice versa! The fact that there is something missing from our language means that it is missing from our character too!"

"Hmmm, that's interesting," I said. "So what is lacking in the Russian character? Lovemaking? Does that mean that Russians don't have sex?" I asked, trying to entrap my wife in the coils of her own argument.

"No, that's not what I mean!" she said. "It's just that we never talk about it. Nice people traditionally don't raise that subject in polite company, and that's why in Russian there's no decent expression equivalent to the English expression *to make love*. And because we are shy as a people the need for such a word has never come up."

"But what about all those wonderful Russian words that begin with the letters ё and e ?" I crowed.

"Oh, those words were created by people when they were drunk. When a Russian gets drunk he opens up and becomes uninhibited and then he makes up rude words for everything," said my wife, and I hastened to write down this conjecture. In my view it is in no way inferior to the opinions of Turgenev, Mérimée, and Engels on the great and mighty Russian language in general, and on the origin of the words given below in particular.

And so, here are the words—or, more exactly—the one

and only word that the Russian language gives us to define lovemaking:

ЕБЛ Я *(yeblia)*

No, that's wrong. Let's try that again, please, with the largest letters we can muster:

ЕБЛЯ

Yes, that's more like it. This word and all the words derived from it adorn fences, walls, stairwells, train and subway cars, school bathrooms, and public toilets in Russia in letters this size and larger. This is how sexually frustrated teenagers declare to the world the irresistible pull that sex exerts over them. A foreigner who comes to Russia for the first time finds these visual aids very helpful in his study of the Russian language. The only difficulty the words present is how they should be translated, since they are not to be found in the dictionaries most often used by scholars and students. To fill the gap, here is a detailed list of other most-often used words.

х у й *(huy)*—prick, dick, cock

п и з д а *(pizda)*—cunt, pussy, twat, quim

ж о п а *(zhopa)*—ass

з а л у п а *(zalupa)*—head of the penis

м а н д а *(manda)*—same as *pizda*

Ельцин жопа! *(Yeltsin zhopa!)* Yeltsin is an ass! (Oops, sorry, now we're getting into political slogans!)

Let's get back to the subject of this chapter, lovemaking, Russian style. Since language really does reflect the character of those who speak it, we need to insert at least a few words about what Russians are like in bed. And the first historical testimony we have once again goes back to the year 922, and comes from Akhmed ibn Fadlan, who wrote:

When the Russians arrive in Khazaria with merchandise from their country, all are struck by their lithe bodies and white skin, covered with outlandish drawings from head to toe, drawings representing birds of prey, beasts and pagan deities. Just as soon as they have docked their brightly painted crafts, each one of them comes ashore bearing bread, meat, onions, milk, and mead. All of this they offer to Velesu, their pagan deity of trade and cattle, who is made of logs and placed in the ground. Bowing before this wooden idol, they say to him, "Oh, my lord, I come from distant lands, and with me I have such-and-such a quantity of girls, and such-and-such a quantity of slaves for sale, and such-and-such a quantity of sables, and so many skins," and thus they list all of the goods that have arrived with them and, placing their gifts before the idol with a human face, they conclude, "And I have come to you with this gift and I hope that you may send me a merchant rich in dinars and dirhem and may he buy everything from me at my asking price." After this they build wooden abodes on the river bank, then lay their merchandise out before them: marten fur, fox fur, squirrel fur, honey and wax, and seat themselves next to it and together with them sit their beautiful girls for the merchants to buy. But soon one of these Russians, without even waiting for a purchaser for his girl or his merchandise, begins to copulate with her himself, and his comrade, looking on him and seeing the girl and the power of her ardor, also feels the desire to copulate rising in him. Sometimes a whole group of them gathers, and they copulate with their females, and when the purchasing merchant finally arrives to buy their merchandise, slave or girl, the Russians cannot trade, because they cannot tear themselves away from their females. . . .

Despite Russian literature's much-vaunted greatness, it is a fruitless task to seek such descriptions in the works of classic writers like Tolstoy, Dostoyevsky, Turgenev, or Chekhov. Count Tolstoy, who was rumored to have had a roll in the hay with practically all of his serf girls, and the great Dostoyevsky, who celebrated the publication of his first novel in a bordello, left their readers not a trace of Russian erotica. For almost two hundred pages Tolstoy prepares us for the moment when Anna Karenina gives herself to Vronsky, but how does the great Tolstoy describe the crucial moment? The entire bedroom scene, the event for which Anna forsakes husband, family, and social position, the moment that Anna dreams of for the entire first part of the novel, the moment when she will get it on with Vronsky, or as Tolstoy himself writes, "that which for almost an entire year had for Vronsky been the sole desire of his life, replacing all his previous desires, that which for Anna had been an impossible, terrible and consequently an even more fascinating dream of happiness—this desire was gratified." And that's it! "Was gratified!" And how was it gratified? In what way? Count Tolstoy, experienced in these matters, hides everything from us, save one insignificant detail, that it happened on a sofa.

> ... she writhed with her whole body and fell from the sofa where she was sitting onto the floor at his feet; she would have fallen on the carpet if he had not supported her. "My God! Forgive me!" she said, gasping, pressing her hands to her breast.... There was something terrible and revolting in the memories of the act which was paid for with this terrible price of shame.

And the reader does not know whether Vronsky was any good or not, and wonders if what happened on that sofa really was something terrible and revolting. If so, then why on earth did Anna trail after Vronsky for another three volumes?

But *real* Russian language, of course, is not so delicate. It goes straight to the heart of the matter, it calls things by their true names. And it has never done anything but.

In the words of Ivan Barkov, a great Russian erotic poet of the eighteenth century:

Без ебли, милая, зачахнешь,
И жизнь те будет не мила!

Bez yebli, milaya, zachakhnesh',
I zhin' te budet ne mila!

If you don't fuck, dear, you will wilt
Good health requires that seed be spilt!

Ебётся вошь, ебётся гнида,
Ебётся тётка Степанида,
Ебётся северный олень,
Ебутся все, кому не лень.
Но боже вас всегда храни
От необузданой ебни!

Yebyotsya vosh', yebyotsya gnida,
Yebyotsya tyotka Stepanida,
Yebyotsya severnyi olen',
Yebutsya vse, komu ne len'!
No bozhe vas vsegda khrani
Ot neobuzdanoy yebni!

The nit, he fucks, so doth the louse,
As doth the lady of the house.
The reindeer fucks,
As do the ducks.
With some luck
We all can fuck.
But may God save both me and you,
From a lewd, crude, rude, licentious screw!

Dermo!

(Isn't this similar to the Cole Porter song, "Let's Do It!"? You remember how that one goes: "Birds do it, bees do it, even educated fleas do it!")

Pushkin, Lermontov, and other Russian poets dedicated many poems to the love act, but we will present here just two of the most popular Russian **частушки** (remember this: **частушки** *chastushki*—folk poems consisting of four lines or two couplets; ditties, in English). We suggest that you learn them by heart:

> **На дворе сирень цветет,**
> **Ветка к ветке клонится.**
> **Парень девушку ебет –**
> **Хочет познакомиться.**

> *Na dvore siren' tsvetyot,*
> *Vetka k vetke klonitsya.*
> *Paren' devushku yebyot –*
> *Hochet posnakomit' sya.*

> The lilacs blossom in the yard,
> In the breeze their branches bend.
> Lad fucks lass, both long and hard.
> And says, "I hope you'll be my friend."

and the second one goes like this:

> **Надень платье синее**
> **И не будь разинею.**
> **Оглянись вокруг себя**
> **Не ебет ли кто тебя.**

> *Naden' plat'e sinaye,*
> *I ne bud' rasinayu.*
> *Oglanis' vokrug sebya*
> *Ne yebyot li kto tebya.*

Put on your blue dress,
Don't be a jerk.
See if someone's fucking you;
Find them where they lurk.

It should be noted that in Russian there is no positive or
even neutral word signifying *oral sex*. The only references to it
are crude expletives such as the following:

Ебаная в рот! *(Yobanaya v rote!)* You suck! Literally,
fucked in the mouth!

В рот тебя ебать! *(V rote tebya ebat'!)* May you be fucked
in the mouth!

В рот ебать твои костыли! *(V rote ebat' tvoyi kostyli!)*
Fuck you in the mouth with your crutches!

When someone wishes to refer to oral sex without judgment or condemnation, they use the French word **минет**
(minet) or the phrases **французская любовь** *(frantsu-
zkaya lyubov'*, literally, *French love)* or **французский
поцелуй** *(fransuskiy potselui*, literally, *French kiss*, but not to
be confused with the English phrase *French kiss* that refers to
kissing with your tongue in your partner's mouth and vice
versa). In the legal context and in court documents to this very
day the term used for oral sex is *sex in a perverted form*. I have
in my possession a copy of a sentence issued in the summer
of 1995 by the People's Court of Moscow to a policeman/
pimp, which reads, "forced [victim] to engage in sex in a perverted form (in the mouth)." From this it is easy to conclude
that even today Russians have a judgmental attitude toward
oral sex.

However, there are positions in sex that have extremely col-
orful descriptions in Russian (Mérimée and Engels did say the

language was expressive, after all!) and are notorious in Russian pop culture:

ебать с погонами *(ebat' s pogonami)*—to fuck with shoulder straps and also

ебать с эполетами *(ebat' s epoletami)*—to fuck with epaulets (both meaning intercourse occurring with the woman's legs on the man's shoulders)

And if one judges by the number of folk sayings and drawings in public toilets on this topic, the most popular position is:

ебать раком *(ebat' rakom)*—to fuck crawfish-style; that is, to enter the woman from the rear, when she is on all fours, a position known in English, of course, as doggy-style

стать раком *(stat' rakom)*—to get into the crawfish position

дать раком *(dat' rakom)*—to give [oneself to someone] in the crawfish position

Even Russian folklore testifies to the popularity of this position in Russia:

Мама, а я шофера люблю!
шофер едет на машине,
Ебёт раком он в кабине –
Мама, я за шофера пойду!

Mama, ya shofyora lyublyu!
Shofer edet na mashine,
Yebyot rakom on v kabine –
Mama, ya za shofyora poidu!

Mama, I'm in love with a guy who drives a truck,
And, oh good lord, is he a glorious fuck!
How he loves to cop a feel,
When he's seated at the wheel,
And he does it crawfish style,
Never slowing down a mile
Just wait till we get married, *then* the brakes will really squeal!

I ought to mention one more term, one that has everything to do with the subject of this chapter:

сломать целку *(slomat' tselku)*—to break the hymen, pop the cherry. (**целку** is from the word **целый** *(tseliy)*, meaning *whole*.)

строить целку *(stroit' tselku)*—to pretend to be a virgin, to play the virgin; used figuratively also means *to be pretentious*.

And finally, here is a term that is specifically Soviet, as it resulted from the housing crisis in Russia that led to chronically overcrowded living conditions:

ебля с перископом *(eblya s periskopom)*—literally, *fucking with a periscope*, meaning to have intercourse in the entryway of an apartment building, crawfish-style, with the woman in front, glancing outside during copulation to make sure that no one is approaching.

In conclusion, here's a recap of words and phrases related to lovemaking, Russian style. Keep it close at hand when you are in Russia—you never know when you may need it.

У вас красивые глаза *(U vas krasiviye glaza)* You have beautiful eyes.

У тебя красивые руки *(U tebya krasiviye ruki)* You have beautiful hands.

У тебя прекрасные волосы *(U tebya prekrasniye volosy)* You have lovely hair.

У тебя замечательный голос *(U tebya zamechatel'niy golos)* You have a wonderful voice.

Давай выпьем! *(Davay vypiem!)* Let's have a drink!

Я пью за тебя! *(Ya piu za tebya!)* I drink to you!

Потанцуем! *(Potantsuem)* Let's dance!

Пойдем ко мне *(Poidyom ko mne)* Let's go to my place.

динамо, крутить динамо *(dinamo, krutit' dinamo)*—to eat and drink at a man's expense and then refuse to sleep with him, not to "put out."

динамистика *(dinamistika)*—a cock tease, prick tease, a woman who parties at a john's expense and then when things start looking like sex, disappears.

только без "динамо," пожалуйста *(tol'ko bez dinamo, pozhalyusta)* No dynamo, please, i.e., I'm paying, so don't run away when it's time for sex.

разденься *(razden'sya)* Undress. (imperative form)

ложись *(lozhis')* Lie down.

кожа, прекрасная кожа, гладкая кожа *(kozha, prekrasnaya kozha, gladkaya kozha)*—skin, lovely skin, smooth skin

волосы, шелковые волосы, льяные волосы, красивые волосы *(volosy, shel'koviye volosy, l'yaniye volosy, krasiviye volosi)*—hair, silky hair, flaxen hair, beautiful hair

грудь *(grud')*—breast(s)

Какая прекрасная грудь! *(Kakaya prekrasnaya grud'!)* What beautiful breasts!

сосок *(sosok)*—nipple

Какой вкусный сосок! *(Kakoy vkusniy sosok!)* What a delicious nipple!

Мне нравится твоя грудь *(Mnye nravitsya tvoya grud')* I like your breasts.

Ой, как мне нравится целовать твою грудь *(Oy, kak mnye nravitsya tselovat' tvoyu grud')* Oh, how I like kissing your breasts.

Раздвинь ноги, пожалуйста *(Razdvin' nogy, pozha-lyuista)* Spread your legs, please.

Еще раздвинь, шире *(Escho razdvin', shire)* Spread them wider.

Боже мой, как я тебя хочу! *(Bozhe moy, kak ya tebya hochu!)* My God, how I want you!

Быстрей, а то я умру! *(Bystraye, a to ya umru!)* Faster, or I'll die!

Разожми ноги, прошу тебя *(Razozhmi nogi, proshu tebya)* Spread your legs, I beg you.

Боже мой, наконец! Господи, как мне хорошо! *(Bozhe moy, nakonets! Gospodi, kak mne horosho!)* My God, finally! Lord, I feel so good!

Какая ты вкусная! *(Kakaya ty vkusnaya!)* You are so delicious! (f.)

Какой ты вкусный! *(Kakoy ty vkusniy!)* You are so deli-cious! (m.)

Боже мой, какой он у тебя большой! *(Bozhe moy, kakoy on u tebya bol'shoy!)* My God, your thing is so big!

Боже мой, какой он горячий! Я уже люблю его! *(Bozhe moy, kakoy on goryachiy! Ya uzhe lublyu evo!)* My God, it's so hot! I love it already! ("It" here is the male organ.)

Дай я его поцелую! *(Dai ya evo potseluyu!)* Let me kiss it!

Быстрей, я хочу его в себя немедленно! *(Bistraye, ya hochu evo v sebya nemedlenno!)* Faster, I want it in me right away!

Не кончай! Не кончай! Не кончай! *(Ne konchay! Ne konchay! Ne konchay!)* Don't come! Don't come! Don't come!

иметь бабу, поиметь женшину *(imet' babu, imet' zhenshinu)*—(literally, *to have a woman*) to sleep with a woman

иметь мужика, поиметь мужчину *(imet' muzhika, poimet' muzhhinu)*—to sleep with a man

употребить бабу *(upotrebit' babu)*—(literally, *to use a woman*) to sleep with a woman

кинуть палку *(kinut' palku)*—(literally, *to toss a stick*) to have a [single] fuck, to get laid, to have a one-night stand

презерватив *(prezervativ)*—official or accepted word meaning *condom*

гондон *(gondon)*—more common word for condom, like the English word *rubber*

Повернись на бок *(Povernis' na bok)* Turn onto your side.

Повернись на спину *(Povernis' na spinu)* Turn onto your back.

Повернись на живот *(Povernis' na zhivot)* Turn onto your stomach.

Нагнись *(Nagnis')* Bend over.

Еще нагнись, ниже! *(Escho nagnis', nizhe!)* Bend over lower!

Боже мой, я умираю! *(Bozhe moy, ya umirayu!)* My God, I'm dying!

Стань спиной и нагнись *(Stan' spinoy i nagnis')* Stand with your back to me and bend over.

62

Dermo!

Повернись ко мне! *(Povernis' ko mne!)* Face me!

Опустись на колени *(Opustis' na koleni)* Get down on your knees.

Стань на колени *(Stan' na koleni)* Get up onto your knees.

поцелуй *(potselui)*—kiss [noun]

целуй *(tselui)*—kiss [verb, imperative]

Целуй клитор *(Tselui klitor)* Kiss my clitoris.

Возьми губами *(Vozmi gubami)* Take it with your lips.

Лижи языком *(Lizhi yazykom)* Lick it [with your tongue].

Возьми в рот *(Voz'mi v rote)* Take it in your mouth.

соси *(sosi)*—suck

заглоти *(zagloti)*—swallow

Заглоти целиком! *(Zagloti tselikom!)* Take the whole thing in your mouth!

Заглоти с яичками! *(Zagloti s yaichkami!)* Take the whole thing in your mouth, and my balls too!

At this point you can switch into English, Chinese, or Portuguese—it doesn't matter any more, you'll be understood!

VII

The New Russians and Their Ever-Expanding Business Lexicon

In 1991 when the Soviet Union had just fallen apart, an acquaintance of mine invited me to his sumptuous suite on Fifth Avenue in New York and proposed a scheme to develop a series of broadcasts for Russian television about how to conduct business under capitalism. He had been a famous performer in Russia before emigrating to the U.S. in the early seventies. In America, he opened an agency handling technical and advertising translation into and from all languages. While he had gotten rich quickly, he had always missed show business and wanted to use a new TV show in Russia to make a comeback. Since the collapse of the Soviet regime, all of Russian television was in the hands of old friends of his, so my friend assumed that all would work out as he planned.

He had in mind a show that would tell Russians how to conduct business properly, explaining what a bank loan is, what a partnership involves, as well as insurance, credit, and so on. There was a real need for a show like this in a country where people lacked a knowledge of the basics—what is a credit card, what are contracts, shares, dividends, stocks, etc. It would be a hit—especially if it were produced in a way that was fun and entertaining, with the best Russian stand-up comedians participating and giving it real entertainment value.

With great excitement we set to work and within a few weeks the show concept and scripts for the first several broadcasts were ready. As a member of the Writers Guild of America and the author of seven Russian feature films, I can assure you that the work that went into all this was very professional. My friend had everything printed on expensive paper and, confident of our idea's imminent success, he flew off to Moscow for negotiations with the network presidents of Moscow television. I never heard from him again.

I'm sure he never had a greater failure in his life. Russians don't want anyone to teach them anything, even business! They would rather spend years reinventing the wheel or the credit card than learn how these things work in the West. This is the reason Russians claim that one of their own—a man by the name of Popov—invented the radio, and that an unknown by the name of Polzunov invented the steam engine. When my first Russian publishers flew to New York to sign a contract with my agent, they stayed at the Park-Lane Hotel in a room that cost twelve hundred dollars a day, and they paid for it in cash! And they asked me, "Edward, how much money do we need to deposit in the bank to get a credit card? Is ten thousand enough?" I tried to explain to them that a credit card is just that, a *credit* card, and that the bank gives you money on *credit*. But anyone who has been in Russia recently can tell you about the credit cards Russians are using now: They deposit money in the bank, and then the bank gives them a plastic so-called credit card for that amount. And as soon as they spend the amount they've deposited, the bank stops its payments on their plastic card.

So the first important piece of advice for anyone planning on doing business deals in Russia is this:
DON'T TRY TO TEACH RUSSIANS HOW TO DO BUSINESS. INSTEAD, LEARN FROM THEM HOW

TO DO BUSINESS RUSSIAN STYLE. Or, to quote a Russian saying, **Со своим уставом в чужой огород не суйся!** (*So svoim ustavom v chuzhoy ogorod ne suysya!—*Don't enforce your own rules on someone else's domain! Or, as we would say in English: When in Rome, do as the Romans do.

The second piece of advice is, never ask a Russian how business is going. While Americans often exaggerate when asked this question, and say, "Great!" Russians are superstitious, and they never say **отлично!** (*otlichno*—great) so as not to jinx things. Instead, they always answer, **так себе!** (*tak sebye*—so-so). He who answers the question *how are things?* by saying **отлично!** (*otlichno*—great) **прекрасно!** (*prekrasno*—fine) **великолепно!** (*velikolepno*—magnificent) is probably just bluffing.

Third piece of advice: never curse in the presence of a Russian who is higher-ranking than you are. Russian functionaries and politicians have the same attitude toward four-letter words that the main character in the movie *Disclosure* has toward sex when he says, "Sex is not about sex, it's about power!" This describes to a tee how Russian bosses at all levels feel about four-letter words. For them four-letter words are not about locker-room talk and male bonding; they are a sign of power, like epaulets and stars on a soldier's uniform. The Boss is the one who is allowed to curse, and no one else! Moving up through the ranks of the *nomenklatura* to the heights of power, Brezhnev, Gorbachev, and the current president put up with the four-letter words of their superiors and did not even have the right to let loose with a mild expletive now and then in their presence. (The only vent they were permitted was to curse even more profanely in the presence of their own subordinates.)

In the last few years the Russian press has written openly that the people surrounding the current president are a cabal of mafiosi consisting of his former Siberian Party flunkies, and while that may be the case, the reason for the president's personal choice is simpler than one might think. The truth is that it's much easier for any president of Russia to communicate directly with his people without having to resort to the tiresome exchange of "would you be so kind as to," and "excuse me, please," and he can do this most comfortably with associates of long standing. Everything is plain, down-to-earth, and working-class, in straightforward Russian style. There is no mincing of words: "Why the fuck didn't you report to me about this sooner, you dick?" "Shithead, do you understand, you bastard, what you've done?!!!" "You whore, I promoted you from fireman to minister, and you shitty scrap of foreskin, you can't even handle the Chechens!" And so on. Of course, in public the head of the country has to restrain himself and instead of words like these he uses meaningless fillers such as "you see," "ummm," and "whatchamacallit." The result is not at all what the speaker intended, but a kind of mishmash. And very few people actually realize that if you replace all this yammering with real ordinary words such as **блядь** (*blyad'*—whore) **ебёнать** (*yobyonat'*—fuck) and **хуй в жопу** (*huy v zhopu*—dick up his ass) that all the speeches of recent Russian leaders immediately take on a new liveliness and color and start to make complete sense. The paradox of the current situation is that nowadays when a politician finally scales the very summit of power, instead of getting what he's earned—the right to swear like a sailor with the entire country as his captive audience—he is forced to choose his words even more cautiously than when he was at the very bottom of the bureaucratic heap. Yes, today any Russian working stiff can yell (and does!) at the top of his lungs on the street, "Our president is a shithead!" but just let the president say the same thing publicly about the workers and see what happens! So some democratic changes *have* in fact taken place in Russia.

This is not, however, a guide to conducting business in

Russia. Our task here is a far more modest one. We are simply introducing you to the specific lexicon of the new Russian businessmen. (I have to say that if the directors of the IMF had learned these words even five years ago they could have saved more than a billion dollars which were poured in the New Russian economy to no avail.)

So, the main words in Russian business today are as follows:

кинуть *(kinut')* or **кидать** *(kidat')* Means literally *to throw*, but is used to mean *to deceive, to screw someone over, to swindle*. This word is crucial, since Russian business deals always involve some sort of deception on both sides. A Russian's business acumen can be measured in terms of his ability to cheat while being cheated (knowing, of course, *how* he is being cheated and taking this into account) and still come out ahead.

Russians have a great sense of humor and are constantly telling jokes on themselves. Here is a joke on precisely the topic we've just been discussing, the business transaction as a form of mutual screwing-over or two-way swindle:

A new Russian businessman has just lost all his money. The devil comes to him and offers to save him from bankruptcy. "So what can you do to help me?" the Russian asks the devil. "Whatever you want!" says the devil. "I can grant any wish! But only on the condition that after you die, your soul becomes mine. Okay?" "Wait!" says the Russian, his mind racing. "What do you mean you can do anything? Can you give me a train car full of aluminum?" "No problem. Right this minute!" answers the devil. "Hmmm ... how about ten railway cars?" "No problem!" "Wait!" the Russian says to the devil once more. "I don't get it: You give me ten railway cars of aluminum *now* and I give you my soul after dying a natural death? Right?" "Exactly right!" "Hmmm!" says the Russian, puzzled and drawing a blank. "I don't get it. What's the catch? How are *you* going to swindle *me*?"

Dermo!

The second great word in new Russian business is:

крыша *(krysha)* Literally, *roof*, used to mean a protector in case of attack by bandits, racketeers, militia, or tax police, i.e., patron or guardian.

Here is a joke on the subject:

A new Russian catches a goldfish. The goldfish begs, "Let me return to the deep blue sea and in exchange I will grant you three wishes." "I want a railway car full of money!" says the Russian. "Sure!" answers the fish, and a railway car full of money falls out of the sky and lands next to the Russian. "I want a railway car filled with gold!" The fish fulfills this one as well. "I want to become the president of Russia!" "Sorry, can't grant that one," says the fish. "The president is my *krysha*."

Here is a list of other Russian new-talk business terms:

наехать *(naekhat')* Literally, *to run over someone in a car*, used now to mean a physical or verbal attack on a business or businessman, in which the latter is forced to pay extortion money. For example, someone might say, **Помоги мне, на меня наехали рэкетиры.** *(Pomogi mne, na menya naekhali reketiri.)* Help me, I've been attacked/approached by racketeers.

разборка *(razborka)* Score settling. Settling an argument or a claim, clarifying differences in a relationship, often with the use of weapons.

базар *(bazar)* Literally, *bazaar* or *farmer's market*, used to mean the same thing as **разборка** *(razborka)*. Also means casual conversation or spoken words.

ответить за базар *(otvetit' za bazar)* To back up one's words/to make good on one's words. For example, someone

might ask the question, **Чем ответишь за базар?**
(Chem otvetish' za bazar?) How are you going to back up or
guarantee your words? And the answer could be, **Чем
хочешь! Вот десять тысяч!** *(Chem khochesh'! Vot
desyat' tysyach!)* However you like! Here's ten grand!

стрелка *(strelka)* Literally means *arrow*, and is also etymo-
logically related to the word for *shooting*. Signifies the location
where score settling (**разборка**/*razborka*) takes place, often,
as already noted, with weapons being used.

Папа Карло *(Papa Carlo)* A stupid person who works
honestly and hard. (Papa Carlo is a character in the fairy
tale "Buratino," a Russian story that bears a suspicious

resemblance to "Pinocchio.") For example: **Вкалывает, как Папа Карло.** (*Vkalyvaet, kak Papa Karlo.*) He toils/works his butt off like Papa Carlo.

карлуешь (*karluesh*) Verb formed from Carlo, "to do a Papa Carlo," "to Carlo it," meaning to work very hard and honestly.

бык (*byk*) Literally, *bull;* term used to designate a rank-and-file gang member who works as a private security guard and carries out dirty work such as attacks, "tax" collection, and so on.

бригадир (*brigadir*) Literally, *foreman;* signifies a person who is in charge of a group of "bulls."

босс (*boss*)—gang leader

отмороженный/отморозок (*otmorozheniy, otmorozok*) Hatchet man; a young "bull" or simply a young man prepared to commit any crime unquestioningly and unthinkingly. Literally, this word means *frostbitten,* i.e., someone who is so stupid and brawny that his brains seem to be frostbitten.

качок (*kachok*) From the word **качать** (*kachat*) *to pump,* means a bodybuilder, someone who pumps iron, a brawny young man with well-developed muscles, usually a hatchet man.

капуста (*kapusta*) Literally means *cabbage;* slang for money, dough.

деревянные (*derevyanniye*) Wooden, refers to Russian rubles, signifying their near-worthlessness. Similar to the English phrase *wooden nickel.*

зеленые (*zelyoniye*)—greens or greenbacks, US dollars

оформить (*oformit'*)—to carry out a scam or fraud

растаможка *(rastamozhka)*—the act of getting merchandise or cargo through customs

Here are some terms that will always be applicable, no matter what changes the Russian economy undergoes:

взятка *(vzyatka)*—bribe

дать в лапу *(dat' v lapu)*—literally, *to put into [someone's] paw*, i.e., to bribe, to grease someone's palm

дать под столом *(dat' pod stolom)*—to give under the table, bribe

зайти с черного хода *(zaiti s chernovo khoda)*—literally, *to go in through the service entrance or the back door*, i.e., to find an illegal means of doing something

смухлевать *(smukhlevat')*—to pull the wool over someone's eyes/to bamboozle

облапошить *(oblaposhit')*—to trick someone out of something, to take someone to the cleaners

обуть *(obut')*—to hoodwink someone out of something, literally, *to put shoes on something* (so that it "walks")

сти брить *(stibrit')*—to steal, to "lift" something

нарисовать ноги *(narisovat' nogi)*—literally, *to draw legs on something*, i.e., to steal, to "walk" something away

зажать *(zazhat')*—to appropriate property belonging to another.

навар *(navar)*—income, profit, "gravy"

моржа *(morzha)*—same as above

бодяга *(bodyaga)*—red tape, busywork

кантоваться *(kantovat'sya)*—to cool one's heels, mark time, wait for something

Dermo!

идёт? *(idyot?)* Will that do? Is it a deal? Shake on it?

идёт! *(idyot!)* It's a deal. Let's shake on it.

But the real secret to getting rich quick is not to be found in the slang the new Russian businessmen coin and use. The key to their money—and big money it is too—lies elsewhere. Let's listen to one of them as he explains it himself in the punch line to this joke (remember this story, as it will come in handy):

A new Russian is driving down the street in his Mercedes when he suddenly sees an old classmate of his sitting on the curb, shabbily dressed, with his hand outstretched, begging. He stops, gets out of the car, walks over to his friend and says, "Kolya, what's this? You were the smartest kid in school! In third grade you were doing square roots in your head without pencil and paper! You got first prize in all the math competitions! You were the valedictorian! You defended your doctoral thesis when you were twenty! What's happened to you? How did you get so poor! What are you doing, panhandling on the street?"

"I just haven't made it in the New Russia," answers the beggar. "But enough about me. Tell me about yourself. You practically flunked out! You could never learn the multiplication tables! They excused you from taking math because you were such a dunce! You didn't even get a diploma, they just gave you a certificate of attendance. Where did you get all this—the Mercedes, the Rolex watch, the Armani trenchcoat?"

"Kolya, it's really very simple," said the New Russian. "I buy cigarettes for a dollar a pack. I sell them for three dollars a pack. And I live on the two percent I make."

So you see, a fancy degree and a highly developed intellect are not the prerequisites for business success in Russia.

VIII
Greetings and Other Important Expressions for Everyday Use

We've been scouting in the murky depths of the Russian language for a while—now let's resurface just briefly. You can drown in even the clearest waters if you stay down too long. And there is more to Russian than four-letter words. After all, even the most foul-mouthed of Russians—even military pilots—have to put *some* decent words in between the expletives.

Greetings

Доброе утро!	*Dobroye utro!*	Good morning!
Привет!	*Privyet!*	Hi!
Салют!	*Salyut!*	Greetings!
Как поживаешь?	*Kak pozhivayesh'?*	How are you?
Как жизнь?	*Kak zhizn'?*	How's life?
Как сам?	*Kak sam?*	And you?

Dermo!

Здорово!	*Zdorovo!*	Great!/Hi! [depending on which syllable is stressed]
Добрый день!	*Dobriy den'!*	Good day!
Мое почтение!	*Moyo pochteniye!*	My respects!
Рад видеть!	*Rad videt'!*	Glad to see you!
Добрый вечер!	*Dobriy vecher!*	Good evening!

If you wish, you can strengthen, lighten, or embellish any of these greetings using the words discussed in previous chapters. For example:

Доброе утро, бля! *(Dobroye utro, blya!)* Good morning, you whore! or: **Доброе утро, душа моя!** *(Dobroye utro, dusha moya!)* Good morning, sweetheart!

Хорошее утро, ёбаный в рот! *(Khoroshee utro, yobaniy v rote!)* Good morning, you cocksucker! (literally, *fucked in the mouth*)

Какое хорошее утро, мой милый! *(Kakoye khoroshee utro, moy miliy!)* What a nice morning, my darling!

Клёвое утро, падла буду! *(Klyovoye utro, padla budu!)* It's a great morning, I'll be damned if it's not!

Клёвое утро, ей богу! *(Klyovoye utro, yea bogu!)* It's a great morning, by God!

Привет! *(Privyet!)* Hi!

Привет, карлуша! *(Privyet karlusha!)* Hi, you ass-buster [hard worker], you!

Привет, братва! *(Privyet, bratva!)* Hi, bros!

Салют! *(Salyut!)* Greetings!

Салют жлобам! *(Salyut zhlobam!)* Greetings, you bums!

Салют красавицам! *(Salyut krasavitsam!)* Greetings, my pretties!

Как поживаешь? *(Kak pozhivayesh'?)* How are you?

Как поживаешь, ёб тать? *(Kak pozhivaeysh', yobe tat'?)* How are you, motherfucker?

Как поживаешь, светик мой? *(Kak pozhivaysh', svetik moy?)* How are you, light of my life?

Как жизнь? *(Kak zhizn'?)* How's life?

Как жизнь, ебёнать? *(Kak zhizn, yobonat'?)* How's life, fucker?

Как жизнь, подруга? *(Kak zhizn', podrooga?)* How's life, my friend (f.)?

Как сам-то, сучий потрох? *(Kak sam-to, suchiy potrokh?)* And you, bitch guts (or, bitch giblets)?

Как сама, душа моя? *(Kak sama, dusha moya?)* And you, my sweetheart?

Здоро́во! *(Zdorovo!)* Hi! **Здоро́во, быки!** *(Zdorovo, byki!)* Hi, bulls!

Здоро́во, коль не шутишь ... *(Zdorovo, kol' ne shutish' . . .)* Hi, and that's no joke . . .

Добрый день! *(Dobriy den'!)* Good day! **День добрый, охламоны!** *(Den' dobriy, okhlamony!)* Good day, you slobs!

Добрый день кому не лень. *(Dobriy den' komu ne len'.)* Good day, if anyone cares/gives a hoot.

Мое почтение! *(Moyo pochteniye!)* My respects!

Мое почтение, мужик! *(Moyo pochteniye, muzhiki!)* My respects, fellas!

Dermo!

Мое почтение, в рот те печение! *(Moyo pochteniye, v rote te pecheniye!)* To you I give my high esteem/and cram in your mouth, a chocolate cream!

Рад видеть! *(Rad videt'!)* Glad to see you!

Рад тя видеть, засранец! *(Rad tya videt', zasranets!)* Glad to see you, filthy bitch!

Рад тя видеть несказанно! *(Rad tya videt neskazanno!)* I can't tell you how glad I am to see you!

Добрый вечер! *(Dobriy vecher!)* Good evening!

Добрый вечер, мать вашу в три креста! *(Dobriy vecher, mat' vashu v tri kresta!)* Good evening, and fuck your mother and three crosses too!

Спокойной ночи! *(Spokoynoy nochi!)* Good night!

Спокойной ночи, малыши! *(Spokoynoy nochi, malyshi!)* Good night, children! [The name of a popular Russian children's television show.]

The brief section below concerns the drinking terms you *must* know to get by in Russia. Drinking is, after all, the most widely practiced indoor sport in the country.

выпивка	*vypivka*	a drinking party, liquor
выпивон	*vypivon*	same
пьянка	*p'yanka*	a drunken revelry;
кир	*kir*	a gathering at which drink is the main entertainment
кирнуть	*kirnut'*	drink, tipple

дерябнуть	*deryabnut'*	drink, slug down
ёбнуть	*yobnut'*	to polish off, demolish (to drink up)
хлобыстнуть	*khlobystnut'*	drink, knock back
врезать	*vrezat'*	to drink [implies large quantities drunk at great speed]
опрокинуть	*oprokinut'*	to turn [a glass] upside down [to drink]
засосать	*zasosat'*	to drink (literally, *to suck up/slurp down*)
бутылка	*butylka*	bottle
бутыль	*butyl'*	bottle
пузырь	*puzyr'*	bottle (slang, literally, *bubble*)
литр	*litr*	liter
литруха	*litrukha*	liter (colloquial)
пол-литра	*pol-litra*	half a liter
чекушка	*chekushka*	a 250-gram bottle
стопарь	*stopar'*	shot glass
закуска	*zakuska*	a snack to accompany vodka—"vodka-chaser"

закусон	*zakuson*	a snack to accompany vodka—"vodka-chaser"
занюхать	*zanyukhat'*	to take a deep whiff of food after drinking (purpose: to provide the drinker with temporary relief from the smell of alcohol without eating, which would diminish the effect of the drink)
стакан	*stakan*	glass

Toasts:

За здоровье!	*Za zdorovye!*	To health!
За счастье!	*Za schastye!*	To happiness!
За удачу!	*Za udachu!*	To luck!
За дружбу!	*Za druzhbu!*	To friendship!
За Россию!	*Za Rossiyu!*	To Russia!
Будем здоровы, а остальное купим!	*Budem zdorovy, a ostal'noye kupim!*	Let's be healthy, everything else we can buy!
За милых дам!	*Za milykh dam!*	To the dear ladies!

Dermo!

За женщин!	*Za zhenschin!*	To women!
За русских женщин!	*Za russkikh zhen-schin!*	To Russian women!
Этим маленьким бокалом, но с большим чувством, я хочу выпить за присутствующих тут дам!	*Etim malen'kim bokalom, no s bol'shim chuvstvom ya khochu vypit' za prisutstvuyuschikh tut dam!*	With this small goblet, but with great feeling, I want to drink for the ladies present here!

EVERYDAY OBJECTS AND WORDS

In your hotel room:

расчёска	*raschoska*	comb
мыло	*mylo*	soap
полотенце	*polotentse*	towel
зубная щётка	*zubnaya shotka*	toothbrush
салфетка	*salfetka*	napkin, Kleenex
зубная паста	*zubnaya pasta*	toothpaste
крем	*krem*	(face) cream
духи	*dukhi*	perfume
одеколон	*odekolon*	eau de cologne
туалет	*tualet*	toilet
душ	*dush*	shower
ванна	*vanna*	bathtub
подушка	*podushka*	pillow

одеяло	*odeyalo*	blanket
простыня	*prostynya*	sheet
кровать	*krovat'*	bed
шкаф	*shkaf*	cupboard
зеркало	*zerkalo*	mirror
отопление	*otopleniye*	heating
кондиционер	*konditsioner*	air conditioner
окно	*okno*	window
комната	*komnata*	room
горничная	*gornichnaya*	maid

Food:

еда	*eda*	food
завтрак	*zavtrak*	breakfast
обед	*obed*	lunch
ужин	*uzhin*	dinner
борщ	*borscht*	beet soup
щи	*schi*	cabbage soup
солянка мясная	*solyanka masnaya*	meat stew
солянка рыбная	*solyanka rybnaya*	fish stew
жаркое	*zharkoye*	roast meat
лангет	*langet*	sliced steak
шашлык	*shashlyk*	shish kebab
котлета	*kotleta*	cutlet or hamburger

мясо	*miaso*	meat
рыба	*pyba*	fish
курица по-киевски	*kuritsa po kievski*	chicken Kiev
бефстроганов	*befstroganov*	beef stroganoff
компот	*kompot*	fruit juice often containing stewed fruit
чай	*chi*	tea
тарелка	*tarelka*	plate
ложка	*lozhka*	spoon
вилка	*vilka*	fork
нож	*nozh*	knife
спички	*spichki*	matches
бокал	*bokal*	wineglass or goblet
стакан	*stakan*	glass
сок	*sok*	juice

Other miscellaneous words:

зажигалка	*zakhigalka*	lighter
папиросы	*papirosy*	cigarettes (often hand-rolled)
сигареты	*sigarety*	cigarettes
деньги	*den'gi*	money
обмен денег	*obmen deneg*	money exchange
рубли	*rubli*	rubles

копейки	*kopeiki*	kopecks
лимон	*lemon*	(literally, *lemon*) a million rubles
такси	*taksi*	taxi
машина	*mashina*	car
улица	*ulitsa*	street
аптека	*apteka*	pharmacy
лекарство	*lekarstvo*	medicine
квартира	*kvartira*	apartment
гостиница	*gostinitsa*	hotel
милиция	*militsiya*	police
милиционер	*militsioner*	policeman
омон	*omon*	special police forces
друг	*droog*	friend
подруга	*podrooga*	friend (f.) or girl-friend
день	*den'*	day
ночь	*noch'*	night
аэропорт	*aeroport*	airport
девушка	*devushka*	girl, "miss"
мужчина	*muzhchina*	man
мальчик	*mal'chik*	boy
девочка	*devochka*	little girl
ребенок	*rebyonok*	child
дети	*deti*	children
снег	*sneg*	snow
дождь	*dozhd'*	rain
свет	*svet*	light

Dermo!

Frequently asked questions:

Сколько стоит? *(Skol'ko stoit?)* How much does it cost?

Почем? *(Pochem?)* How much?

Кто крайний? *(Kto krainiy?)* Who's last in line?

Когда начало? *(Kogda nachalo?)* When does it start?

Который час? *(Kotoriy chas?)* What time is it?

Сколько время? *(Skol'ko vremya?)* What time is it?

Как пройти в . . . ? *(Kak proitee v . . . ?)* How do I get to . . . ?

Как попасть на . . . улицу? *(Kak popast' na . . . ulitsu?)* How do I get to . . . Street?

Как вас звать? *(Kak vas zvat'?)* What is your name?

Где вы живёте? *(Gde vy zhivyote?)* Where do you live?

Вы замужем? *(Vy zamuzhem?)* Are you married? [addressed to a woman]

Вы женаты? *(Vy zhenati?)* Are you married? [addressed to a man]

У вас есть друг? *(U vas est' droog?)* Do you (formal) have a (boy)friend?

У тебя есть подруга? *(U tebya est' podruga?)* Do you (informal/singular) have a (girl)friend?

Several common phrases:

Куда пойдем? *(Kuda poidyom?)* Where will we go? (on foot)

Куда поедем? *(Kuda poyedem?)* Where will we go? (in a vehicle)

Я хочу вас пригласить. *(Ya khochu vas priglasit'.)* I want to invite you.

Я хочу вам помочь. *(Ya khochu vam pomoch'.)* I want to help you.

Спасибо. *(Spasibo.)* Thank you.

Пожалуйста. *(Pozhalyusta.)* Please.

Позвольте ваше пальто, мадам. *(Pozvol'te vashe pal'to, madam.)* Allow me, your coat, madam. **Позвольте мпе подать вам ваше пальто, мадам** *(Pozvol'te mne podat' vam vashe pal'to madam.)* Allow me to give you your coat, madam.

Извини те. *(Izvineetye.)* Excuse me.

Простите. *(Prosteetye.)* Forgive me.

Это моя вина. *(Yeto moya vina.)* It is my fault.

Позвольте. *(Pozvol'te.)* Allow me.

Разрешите. *(Razresheetye.)* Permit me.

С удовольствием! *(S udovol'stviem!)* With pleasure!

Разрешите закурить! *(Razresheetye zakurit')* Permit me to have a smoke

Позвольте прикурить. *(Pozvol'te prikurit'.)* Could you give me a light?

Позвольте представиться. *(Pozvol'te predstavit'sya.)* Permit me to introduce myself.

Разрешите познакомиться. *(Razresheetye poznakomit' sya.)* Allow me to introduce myself.

Dermo!

Могу ли я пригласить вас к себе в гости? *(Mogu li ya priglasit' vas k sebe v gosti?)* May I invite you to come and visit me?

Помогите мне! *(Pomogeetye mne!)* Help me!

Спасите! *(Spaseetye!)* Save me!

Вы мне нравитесь. *(Vy mne nravites'.)* I like you.

Ты мне очень нравишься. *(Ty mne ochen' nravish'sya.)* I like you very much.

Я тебя люблю. *(Ya tebya lyublyu.)* I love you.

Useful tips:

When addressing a police officer (taxi driver, porter, concierge, doorman, and even a waiter) the best form of address is

командир *(komandir)*—literally, *commander*

When addressing a woman whom you do not know, you may call her

дорогая *(dorogaya)*—dear

девушка *(devushka)*—girl or miss

сударыня *(sudarynya)*—madam

барышня *(baryshnya)*—mademoiselle

When addressing a man whom you don't know, call him one of the following:

мужчина *(muzchina)*—man

дорогой *(dorogoy)*—dear

сударь *(sudar')*—sir

молодой человек *(molodoy chelovek)*—young man

друг *(droog)*—friend

Forms of address used among common folk:

милок *(milok)*—dear

керя *(kerya)*—friend, buddy

кореш *(koresh)*—pal

браток *(bratok)*—"bro' "

Impersonal forms of address used in more exalted circles:

Будьте добры! *(Bud'te dobry!)* Be kind; do me a favor!

Пожалуйста! *(Pozhalyusta!)* Please!

Будьте любезны! *(Budte lubezniy!)* Be gracious (and do me a favor).

Вы не могли бы мне помочь? *(Vy ne mogly bui mne pomoch'?)* Could you help me?

A common way of requesting service: **Друг, выручи!** *(Droog, vyruchi!)* Friend, give me a hand!

Будь другом, помоги! *(Bud' droogom, pomogi!)* Be a pal / friend, help out!

Dermo!

Seventeen commandments from the newspaper *Nedelya* [The Week]:

The popular Moscow weekly **Неделя** *(Nedelya)* published twenty-eight commandments for foreigners visiting the Russian capital for the first time. We have reprinted the most useful of them here:

1. Do not buy liquor at kiosks on the street.
2. Do not buy more than two or three items in large stores or department stores. Everything else you should buy in the smaller stores—the quality will be the same and the prices will be much lower.
3. Avoid gypsies, do not give money to beggars in the subway or in train stations, do not participate in any lotteries or street games (such as cockroach races, etc.). You will very quickly find yourself with empty pockets.
4. Learn to read the subway map. It is simple.
5. Trust no one. Never get into conversations with people you don't know. Try to avoid talking with Muscovites.
6. Pay attention, be efficient, nervy, and rude. Don't let anything surprise you. Try not to look like a person of means. Walk quickly and don't get in people's way.
7. Eat ice cream. It is the best thing Moscow has to offer.
8. Do not change hard currency on the street with anyone.
9. Visit Red Square, McDonald's, take a stroll on the Arbat, stop by the Tretyakov Gallery and a nightclub with live music and go roller-skating in Gorky Park. And visit at least one beer hall.
10. Don't be afraid of Muscovites; they are weird but not dangerous.
11. Don't take taxis, it is more expensive than hitching a ride for money with a private driver (in Russia almost everyone who has a car operates on the side as an informal car service).

12. Don't shop at the farmers' markets, and if you do go to one, hang on to your wallet, watch your pockets, and leave as soon as you can.

13. Write down the address and telephone number of the place where you are staying and keep them with you at all times.

14. Keep in mind that the subway does not run at night.

15. Come here to live.

16. Get out of here. We're sick of you.

17. Leave as soon as you can; if you stay too long, you'll get used to Moscow and then you'll be miserable when you go home because you'll miss it so much.

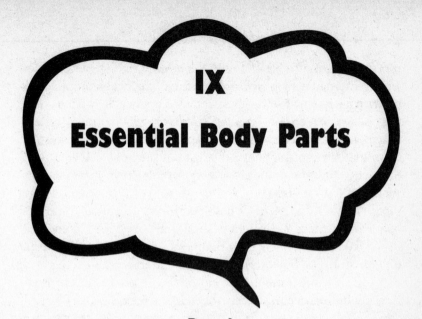

IX
Essential Body Parts

Part I

We promised to raise your knowledge of the great and mighty Russian language up to the third tier. Now we shall get on with the task. As you learned in the first chapter, the most important and, shall we say, basic word in the Russian language is the word мать *(mat')*. If you know this word and even ten expressions that include it (ёб твою мать! / *yob tvoyu mat'!* мать твою перемать! / *mat' tvoyu peremat'!* мать твою растуды! / *mat' tvoyu rastudy!* and so on) then you have covered the basics and laid the foundation for a broader knowledge of Russian. And a very sturdy foundation it is—in fact, it is capable of bearing the weight of up to a hundred tiers! So give it a try!

The second most widely used word in live Russian speech is, without a doubt, the great and simple хуй (*huy*—prick, penis, dick, cock). It is this word that greets you first on the wall of Moscow's Sheremetevo International Airport and subsequently provides a sight for sore eyes as it peeps or peers out from virtually all fences and walls in Russia. Unfortunately, the *Russian Dictionary of Word Frequencies*, which determines which Russian words are used most often, was compiled by **очкарики** (*ochkariki*—bespectacled eggheads), **гнилыми интеллигентами** (*gnilymi intelligentami*—rotten intellectuals) and **скопцами** (*skoptsami*—eunuchs or castratos) from the Russian Language Institute of the Soviet Academy of Sciences, and they stuck some miserable little conjunctions such as **а** (*but*) **и** (*and*) **от** (*from*) and so on in first place as the most frequently used. These pathetic so-called linguists believe that these meaningless sounds are the most often used in the Russian language. But that is an unadulterated lie, based on the study of bowdlerized Russian literature. Of course if you squeeze, sift out, and get rid of all the profanities in Russian, including even innocent ones like **яйца** (*yaytsa*—Literally, *eggs*, but meaning *balls*, or *nuts*, as in *testicles*) **попочка** (*popochka*—little derriere/butt) then of course it is the faceless interjections that pull ahead and take first place. But if you conduct a statistical analysis of *real* Russian speech, then there is no doubt that the words to occupy the front ranks will be: **мать** (*mat'*) **хуй** (*huy*—dick) **пизда** (*pizda*—cunt) **ебать** (*ebat'*—to fuck) and **жопа** (*zhopa*—ass).

In this chapter we will study these prizewinners and terms derived from them. A person who learns even one third of this lexicon can be sure of being the most popular and honored foreigner at any Russian gathering, whether it is a group of drunken bums in Gorky Park or some high muckety-mucks in the president's offices on the third floor of the Kremlin.

Let us begin with that beloved Russian word **хуй**. See what a magnificent bouquet—no, not a bouquet, an entire garden!—has grown from this tiny root of just three letters! What shoots and tendrils, what buds, flowers and entire branches, groaning with the weight of leaves and blossoms! Just take a look:

хуй *(huy)*—prick, cock, dick

х . ** *(h.)* This is how the word **хуй is represented in literary works.

ху *(hu)*—euphemism for *huy*

хуек *(huyok)*—pecker, little prick

хуечек *(huyechek)*—a tiny prick, weenie

хуишко *(huyishko)*—wee-wee, pee-pee, a teeny-weeny prick, deserving of contempt

хуйло *(huylo)*—a large prick, tool, rod

хуй в очках *(huy v ochkakh)*—an intellectual man (literally, *a prick in spectacles*)

хуй маринованный *(huy marinovanniy)*—a marinated prick, an expletive signifying an inert, limp person who takes no initiative

хуй моржовый *(huy morzhoviy)*—literally, *a walrus prick*, an expletive meaning bonehead or jerk

хуёвина *(huyovina)*—something worthless or ridiculous; can mean pretty much whatever the speaker intends; for example:

1. Ничего толкового не могу писать-сплошная хуёвина получается. *(Nichevo tolkovovo ne mogy pisat'-sploshnaya huyovina poluchaetsa.)* I can't write anything worthwhile—I keep producing pure garbage.
2. Взял эту хуёвину, пришел домой, поставил в вазу. *(Vzyal etu huyevinu, prishel domoy, postavil v vazu. . . .)* So I took this crap, came home, and stuck it in a vase. . . .

хуёво *(huyovo)*—lousy, bad. Example: **Хуёвые твои дела, старик!** *(Huyoviye tvoyi dela, starik!)* Things are shitty/aren't looking good for you, old man!

хуевато *(huyevato)*—sort of bad

хулиган *(huligan)*—from the Irish *hooligan*; someone who misbehaves, uses foul language or disturbs the peace

хуеглот *(huyeglot)*—literally, *prick swallower*, used to mean a bad person, a louse

хуесос *(huyesos)*—literally, *a cocksucker*, used to mean a good-for-nothing, a scoundrel

хуё-моё *(huyo-moyo)*—this and that. Example: **Встретил друга, хуё-моё, поговорили, и пошли в магазин за бутылкой.** *(Vstretil drooga, huyo-moyo, pogovorili i poshli v* *magazine za butylkoy.)* I met a friend, we talked about this and that (bullshitted, shot the shit, shot the breeze) and went to the store to get some booze.

А ху-ху не хо-хо? *(a hu-hu ne ho-ho?)*—used replaceably with **А хуя не хочешь?** (*"A huya ne hochesh?"* which means, "You don't want a prick, do you?") that is, "Are you looking for a punch in the nose?" or "Are you cruising for a bruising?" or simply, "Go fuck yourself."

Хуй в жопу! *(Huy v zhopu!)*—literally, *a prick up your ass!* means a refusal, "Nothing doing!" "Not on your life!" "Fat chance!"

хуй в шляпе *(huy v shlyape)*—literally, *a hat-wearing prick,* meaning any person wearing a hat and passing himself off as an intellectual.

хуй его знает *(huy evo znayet)*—"prick knows," i.e., Who the fuck knows.

хуй на палочке *(huy na palochke)*—literally, *prick on a stick,* an insult usually applied to a skinny man.

Хуй с ним! *(Huy s nim!)* To hell with it; also signifies agreement to someone else's conditions.

Хуй с тобой! *(Huy s toboy!)*—literally, *dick with you!* meaning, the hell with it! Signifies agreement. Example: **Мне это не совсем выгодно, но хуй с ним, я согласен!** *(Mne eto ne sovsem vygodno, no huy s nim, ya soglacen!)* It's not quite favorable for me, but the hell with it, I'll go along with it!

Хуй тебе! *(Huy tebe!)*—prick to you! a total, categorical refusal

Хуй тебе в глаз! *(Huy tebe v glaz!)*—literally, *a prick in your eye.* A simple insult, usually an expression of irritation or annoyance.

Хуй тебе в жопу! *(Huy tebe v zhopu!)*—literally, *a prick up your ass!* An insult, usually accompanying a categorical refusal of something.

до хуя *(do huya)* 1. a lot of something, plenty. Example: **В магазине водки до хуя!** *(V magazine vodki, do huya!)* The store has vodka up the wazoo/shitloads of vodka. 2. indifference. Example: **Мне это до хуя, неинтересно!** *(Mne eto do huya, neinteresno!)* I don't give a flying fuck!

по хуй *(po huy)*—indifference. Example: **Мне это по хуй!** *(Mne eto po hui!)* See above.

На хуя? *(Na huya?)* What for? Example: **Тебе это на хуя?** *(Tebe eto na huya?)* What the fuck do you need that for? You need that like you need a hole in the head.

Один хуй! *(Odin huy!)* It's all the same; six of one and half a dozen of the other. Example: **Мне что ехать, что идти—один хуй не успею!** *(Mne shto ekhat', chto idti-odin huy ne uspeyu!)* I don't give a fuck whether we walk or drive—I won't get there in time either way!

ни хуя! *(ni huya!)*—zero, zip, naught, nothing, not worth shit. Example: **Сколько не старался—ни хуя не вышло!** *(Skol'ko ne staral'sya-ni huya ne vyshlo!)* No matter how hard I worked, I didn't get shit—nothing worked! Or this wonderful example from the poetry of the great Russian poet Alexander Pushkin:

> От холода себя страхуя,
> Купил сибирскую доху я.
> Купив доху, дал маху я –
> Доха не греет ни хуя!

> *Ot holoda sebya strakhuya,*
> *Kupil sibirskuyu dokhu ya.*

Dermo!

Kupiv dokhu, dal makhu ya –
Dokha ne grayet ne huya!

I was as cold as a witch's tit
So I bought a Siberian fur.
That fur coat didn't warm me worth shit
My cock froze hard and I still said "brrr!"

ни хуя особенного *(ni huya osobennovo)*—nothing in particular

хоть бы хуй! *(khot' by huy!)*—nothing, nothing happened
Example: **Упал с третьего этажа – и хоть бы хуй, даже не ушибся!** *(Upal s tret'evo etazha – i khot' by huy, dazhe ne ushibsya!)* I fell from the third floor, but nothing happened—I didn't even get a fucking bruise!

Соси хуй! *(Sosi huy!)*—literally, *go suck dick!* a refusal

сосать хуй *(sosat' huy)*—literally, *to suck dick;* means to be poverty stricken, to have nothing.

с гулькин хуй *(s gul'kin huy!)*—almost nothing, a meaningless quantity, peanuts. Example: **Вкалывал целый день, работал как Папа Карло, а получил с гулькин хуй!** *(Vkalyval tseliy den', rabotal kak Papa Karlo, a poluchil s gul'kin huy!)* I worked my butt off all day, and I made chickenshit!

На хуй! *(Na huy!)*—to hell with you! refusal

посылать на хуй *(posylat' na huy)*—to curse someone, to give them what for, using the word **хуй**. Literally, *to send someone to the dick.*

хуйня *(huynya)*—nonsense, stupidity, absurdity

хуярить *(huyarit')*—to do something painstakingly, or to beat someone

хуячить *(huyachit')*—to beat someone

не хухры-мухры *(ne huhry-muhry)*—something not insignificant. Example: **Это тебе не хухры-мухры** *(Eto tebe ne huhry-muhry)*. This is not chopped liver/no small potatoes. This is something serious.

вхуячить *(vhuyachit')*—to hit, to light into someone

Захуячить/захуярить *(zahuyachit'/zahuyarit')*—to hit with all your strength, to whale on someone or something, to take a swing at, to throw somewhere, heave.

нахуярить/нахуячить *(nahuyarit'/nahuyachit')*—to make a lot of something, to produce excess. Example: **Он этих гвоздей нахуярил целую гору!** *(On etikh gvozday nahuyaril tseluyu goru!)* He produced shitloads of nails, a mountain of them!

нахуяриться/нахуячиться *(nahuyarit'sya/nahuyachit' sya)* 1. to get drunk; 2. to overwork oneself to the point of utter exhaustion, to work one's butt off.

остохуеть *(ostohuyet')*—to bore, to make a pest of oneself. Example: **Отъебись от меня, ты мне остохуел!** *(Ot'ebis' ot menya, ty mne ostohuyel!)* Fuck off, you bore me/I've had it with you.

охуеть/охуевать *(ohuyet'/ohuyevat')* 1. to be puzzled; 2. to be amazed; 3. to go nuts/crazy; 4. to be impressed.

охуительно *(ohuitel'no)*—to an extreme degree. Examples: **1. Вошла баба охуительной красоты, принцесса!** *(Voshla baba ohuitel'noy krasoti, printsessa!)* In walked a mind-blowingly beautiful chick, a princess. **2. Это просто охуительный урод, настоящий Квазимодо!** *(Eto prosto ohuitel'noy urod, nastoyaschiy Kvasimodo!)* He is just incredibly ugly, a real Quasimodo!

охуевающе *(ohuyeviyusche)*—terrific, fantastic, stupefying, mind-boggling

отхуячить *(othuyachit')*—to beat (someone) up

похуячить *(pohuyachit')*—to go somewhere, overcoming obstacles and difficulties in the process. Example: **Ему сказали дойти пешком до Амура, и он похуячил!** *(Emu skazali doiti peshkom do Amura, i on pohuyachil!)* They told him to go to the Amur (a river in Siberia) on foot, and I'll be damned if he didn't make it there!

расхуячить *(razhuyachit')*—to break, to shatter, smash. Example: **На хуй ты эту вазу расхуячил?** *(Na huy ty etu vasu rashuyachil?)* What the fuck did you smash that vase for? Or, still better yet: **На хуй ты эту хуевину расхуячил?** *(Na huy ty etu huyachinu razhuyachil?)* What the fuck did you smash [fuck] up that fucking thingamajig for?

Now imagine if you can, an employee of the American undercover radio broadcast interception service who doesn't understand Russian cursing and overhears the following conversation between two Russian pilots (transcription and translation follow):

FIRST PILOT:	**Ты что, охуел? На хуя ты эту хуевину хуячишь?**
SECOND PILOT:	**А хули?**
FIRST:	**Ты что, с хуя сорвался? Это же Белый Дом, бля!**
SECOND:	**А хуи с ним! Давай еще и по этой залупе пизданем!**
FIRST:	**По какой?**
SECOND:	**Да вот по этой залупе с куполом!**
FIRST:	**Мудак! Это у них называется Конгресс, бля!**
SECOND:	**А мне по хуй! Сейчас ёбну и пиздец! А то зенки слепит!**

FIRST PILOT: *Ty shto, ohuyel? Na huya ty etu huyevinu huyachish?* (Are you fucked up or what? What the fuck are you banging on that shit for?)

SECOND PILOT: *A huli?* (Why the fuck not?)

FIRST PILOT: *Ty shto, s huya sorvalsya? Eto zhe Beliy Dom, blya!* (Are you nuts? Literally: *Have you been torn off your dick?* That's the White House, you asshole!)

SECOND PILOT: *A huy s nim! Davai esche po etou zalupe pisdanyom!* (Fuck it! Let's cunt [bash] that dickhead again!)

FIRST PILOT:	*Po kakoy?* (Which one?)
SECOND PILOT:	*Da bot po etou zalupe s kupolom!* (That dickhead with the dome on top.)
FIRST PILOT:	*Mudak! Eto u nikh nazyvaetsya Kongress, blya!* (Jerk-off! That's the Congress, asshole!)
SECOND:	*A mne po huy! Saychas yobnu i pizdetz! A to zen'ki slepit!* (I don't give a flying fuck! I'll fuck it [whack it] right now and it'll be a cunt [cool/hot shit]! It's so bright it's hurting my eyes!)

And so on and so forth. What will the radio interceptor make of this if he doesn't understand Russian four-letter words?

Sayings and Set Phrases

На хуя попу гармонь? *(Na huya popu garmon'?)* What the fuck does a priest need an accordion for? Meaning: What do I need that for? I need that like a fish needs a bicycle/ like I need a hole in the head.

На хуй нищих-Бог подаст. *(Na huy nischikh-Bog podast.)* Fuck the poor, God will help them. (Let 'em eat cake.) A refusal to make a contribution or perform an act of selflessness.

Не хуй выёбываться. *(Ne huy vyobyvat'sya.)* There is no reason to show off/what are you prancing around/preening for?

Ни хуя себе. *(Ni huya sebe.)* An exclamation signifying amazement: Well, how do you like that!/Well, I'll be god-damned! Example: **Ни хуя себе обед ты сьел! три тарелки супа и шесть котлет!** *(Ni huya sebe obed ty s'el! tri tarelki supa i shest kotlet!)* That was some fucking lunch you put away: Three bowls of soup and six hamburgers!

Dermo!

На чужом хую в рай не поедешь. *(Na chuzhom huyu v rai ne poedesh'.)* You won't make it to heaven on someone else's dick. Meaning: You won't be rewarded for someone else's good work. Or: you can't sponge off other people.

Пусть мне хуй на пятаки порубают. *(Pust' mne huy na pyataki porubayut.)* May they cut my dick into pieces and make coins out of them [if I am telling a lie] (this is an oath).

с хуя сорвался *(s huya sorvalsya)* To be torn off one's dick, meaning: To show up unexpectedly without warning, or to go nuts, to go off your rocker.

ноль целых хуй десятых *(nul' tselykh huy desyatykh)* Zero wholes and prick tenths/zero point prick. Meaning: A big fat zero, zilch.

хуем груши околачивать *(huyem grushi okolachivat')* Literally, *to take a swing at pear trees with your dick* [so that pears will fall down, presumably], meaning: To hang out and be idle, to twiddle your thumbs, contemplate your navel.

Ditty:

> **Мы не сеем и не пашем,**
> **А валяем дурака:**
> **С колокольни хуем машем –**
> **Разгоняем облака!**
>
> *My ne seyem i ne pashem,*
> *A valyaem duraka.*
> *S kolokol'ni huyem mashem –*
> *Razgonyaem oblaka!*
>
> We don't reap, neither do we sow,
> We just wag our dicks to and fro.
> Thus we chase the clouds away,
> And act like fools the livelong day!

Other words used to replace the word **хуй** *(huy)*:

хрен *(hren)*—literally, *horseradish*

хер (pronounced like English word *hair*)—means same thing as *huy*

фуй *(fuy)*—euphemism for **хуй** *(huy)*

The three words and expressions given above may be used to replace **хуй** *(huy)*. For example, instead of saying **На хуя попу гармонь?** *(Na huya popu garmon'?*—What the fuck does the priest need an accordion for?), you can say, **На хера попу гармонь?** *(Na haira popu garmon'?)* and it means the same thing, although not as rude. And **На хрен ты эту хреновину расхерачил?** *(Na hren ty etu hrenovinu ras-herachil?)* means the same thing as **На хуй ты эту хуевину расхуячил?** *(Na huy ty etu huyovinu ras-huyachil?)*, i.e., "What the fuck did you fuck up [break] that fucking thing for?"

Part 2

Пизда! *(pizda)* The cunt! Living's sweetest pleasure! . . .
—Popular poem

The word **пизда** *(pizda)*, which may be translated variously as *cunt, pussy, twat, beaver, quim,* and other words too numerous to list here, is the third most frequently used word in Russian after **мать** *(mat')* and **хуй** *(huy)*, although significantly more poems and verses are dedicated to it than to all Russian mothers and penises combined. The line that we have taken as the epigraph of this section is attributed to Gavril Derzhavin, father of Russian poetry and teacher of Pushkin. Here is the verse in its entirety:

> Пизда! – О жизни наслажденье,
> Пизда – вместилище утех,
> Пизда – небес благословенье,
> Пизде и кланяться не грех.
>
> *Pizda! – O zhizni naslazhden'e,*
> *Pizda – vmestilische utekh,*

Pizda – nebes blagosloven'e,
Pizde i klanyat'sya ne grekh.

The cunt is living's sweetest pleasure.
The cunt's an ample box of treasure.
Whenever a cunt happens my way,
I go down on my knees and to that cunt I pray.

There have been many attempts to outdo this poetic paean to the pussy, but in my view none have been successful, except perhaps this gem of folk humor from Catherine the Great's time:

Что ваша Польша!
У нашей Екатерины одна пизда больше!

Shto vasha Pol'sha!
U nashay Yekateriny odna pizda bol'she!

Catherine the Great had such a large twat
Compared to it, Poland's a minuscule dot.

And here is the linguistic bouquet created from this word:

пизда *(pizda)*—cunt, pussy, twat, quim

п . . . *(p . . .)*—abbreviation of the word **пизда** *(pizda)*, used in books

пиздёнка *(pizdyonka)*—little cunt

пиздушка *(pizdushka)*—little cunt

пиздятина *(pizdyatina)*—large cunt

пиздище *(pizdische)*—very large cunt

пиздануть *(pizdanut')* 1. to strike; 2. to steal

пизданутый *(pizdanuty)*—downtrodden, pussy-whipped, beaten down, abnormal, silly

пизданутый на голову *(pizdanuty na golovu)*—silly, stupid (*pizdanuty* literally, *in the head*)

пиздень *(pizden')*—nonsense. Example: **Вот такая пиздень весь день!** *(Vot takaya pizden' ves' den'!)* Meaning: And this is the kind of crap I've been getting all day!

пиздец *(pizdets)*—the end, a fiasco, a flop

пиздеть *(pizdet')*—to talk a big line, lie, brag, bluster, be a blowhard

пиздёж *(pizdyozh)*—fibbing, bullshit

пиздобратия *(pizdobratiya)*—a group of friends (literally, a *cunt-brotherhood*)

пиздорванец/пиздорванка *(pizdorvanets/pizdorvanka)*—wretch (m./f.) or (in the case of a woman) a woman of loose morals, or simply any woman

пиздоёб *(pizdoyob)*—asshole, literally, *cunt-fucker*

пиздодуй *(pizdoduy)*—literally, *cunt-blower;* means a romantic man who is attractive to women; sweet-talker, Romeo

пиздёныш *(pizdyonysh)*—a runt, a small person, a child, someone who is puny and insignificant

припиздёныш *(pripizdyonysh)*—a small downtrodden person, wimp

припизданутый *(pripizdanuty)*—stupid

пиздюк *(pizdyuk)*—scoundrel

пиздострадатель *(pizdostradatel')*—literally, *cunt-sufferer,* meaning a man who chases women and is constantly aroused and seeking satisfaction or sexually frustrated; a satyr

запиздярить *(zapizdyarit')*—to do/make something or to throw something; to hit. Example: **Я ему такой обед запиздярила, а он поел и уснул!** *(Ya emu takoy obed zapizdyarila, a on poel i usnul!)* I whipped up such a great lunch for him, and he ate and then dropped off to sleep! Or: **Он в меня тарелкой как запиздярит!** *(On v menya tarelkoy kak zapizdyarit!)* He'll just take a plate and let it fly at me!

запиздячить *(zapizdyachit')*—same as **запиздярить** *(zapizdyarit')*

опизденеть *(opizdenet')*—to go into a frenzy, to lose it, to fly off the handle

остопиздеть *(ostopizdet')*—to bore someone, to make them sick of you, to get on their nerves. Example: **Вы мне остопиздели своими уроками вежливости!** *(Vy mne ostopizdeli svoimi urokami vezhlivosti!)* I'm fed up with you and your lessons in polite behavior!

отвесить пиздюлей *(otvesit' pizdulay)*—to beat up, to punch in the face

отпиздить *(otpizdit')*—to beat up

отпиздячить/отпиздярить *(otpizdyachit'/otpizdyarit')*—to beat up

припиздеть *(pripizdet')*—to embroider (a story), to add fictional details

распиздяй *(raspizdyai)*—an unreliable, undisciplined, sloppy person, a fuck-up

спиздить *(spizdit')*—to steal

пиздюхать *(pizdyukhat')*—to schlep, to drag oneself. Example: **Далеко нам еще пиздюхать?** *(Daleko nam escho pizdyukhat'?)* Do we still have far to schlep?

Synonyms for **пизда** (*pizda*) cunt:

шахна (*shakhna*)

дырка (*dyrka*)—literally, *little hole*

лоханка (*lokhanka*)

лохматка (*lokhmatka*)—muff or bush (literally, *little shaggy one*)

манда (*manda*)

вагина (*vaggina*)

шмонка (*shmonka*)

щелка (*schelka*)—slit

Expressions and sayings:

пизда маринованная (*pizda marinovannaya*)—an epithet; literally, *marinated cunt*; means a limp, droopy, inert woman

пизда старая (*pizda staraya*)—old cunt, means an old woman

пизда с зубами (*pizda s zubami*)—a cunt with teeth; means *nasty bitch*

пизда рваная (*pizda rvanaya*)—tattered or torn cunt (epithet)

дать по пизде (*dat' po pizde*)—to hit; literally, *to give it to someone in the cunt*

до пизды! (*do pizdy!*)—signifies indifference. Example: **Мне ваши уроки до пизды!** (*Mne vashi uroki do pizdy!*) I don't give a flying fuck about your homework!

до пизды дверцы (*do pizdy dvertsy*)—used to emphasize the futility of something, or one's indifference to something. Example: **Ей это нужно как прошлогодний**

снег, как до пизды дверцы! (*Yei eto nuzhno, kak proshlogidnii sneg, kak do pizdy dvertsy!*) She needs that like last year's snow, like a cunt needs doors! (She doesn't give a fuck!)

пиздой накрыться (*pizdoy nakryt'sya*) Literally, *to be covered with cunt*, meaning to be a total loss. Example: **И этот день пиздой накрылся, а что сделано мной для человечества?** (*I etot den' pizdoy nakrylsya, a shto* *sdelano mnoy dlya chelovechestva?)* This day has been a total loss; what contribution to humanity have I made today?

пиздой торговать *(pizdoy torgovat')* Literally, *to trade* or *deal in cunt*; meaning to engage in prostitution

пизду смешить *(pizdu smeshit')* Literally, *to make cunt laugh*; meaning to talk bullshit

пиздуй отсюда! *(pizdui otsyuda!)* Get the hell out of here!

послать в пизду на переделку *(poslat' v pizdu na peredelku)* to tell someone to go to hell, to send someone packing, to go to hell in a handbasket

с пизды свалиться *(s pizdy svalit'sya)* Literally, *to fall out of a cunt*; meaning to appear unexpectedly, to be unprepared for something, to be born yesterday. Example: **Как ты мог этого не знать? ты что – с пизды свалился?** *(Kak ty mog etovo ne znat'? Ty shto – s pizdy svalilsya?)* How could you not know that! Did you just fall out of a cunt?

Не пизди *(Ne pizdi!)*—literally, *Don't cunt!* Meaning: stop lying!

пизда-разбойница *(pizda-razboynitsa)*—a loose, profligate woman, literally, *gangster cunt* or *outlaw cunt*

на пиздятинку потянуло *(na pizdatinku potyanulo)*— literally, *to feel an urge for a bit of cunt*; meaning to get horny

по глазам-целка, по пизде-блядь *(po glazam tselka, po pizde, blyad')*—literally, *has the eyes of a virgin and the cunt of a whore*, i.e., a slutty young thing with innocent eyes; Madonna-whore

ни в пизду, ни в красную армию *(ni v pizdu, ne v krasnuyu armiyu)*—literally, *neither in the cunt nor in the Red Army*; means someone who's not good for anything. He doesn't know his ass from first base/from his elbow/shit from Shinola.

This last phrase was created relatively recently (judging by the reference to the Red Army) and yet how wonderfully expressive it is!

Part 3

Everyone in the world loves a good joke, a unique witticism, a well-timed bon mot. I am sure that if there was such a thing as an international Olympic competition among experts in expletives and profanity, the Russian championship would garner more spectators than a hockey match! And the team could demonstrate that the word **жопа** (*zhopa*—ass) alone can embody the amazingly flexible, metaphorical, and vivid qualities of the Russian language. Here are just a few examples:

жополиз (*zhopoleez*)—literally, *ass licker*; as in English, it means brownnoser, toady, sycophant

жопник (*zhopnik*)—rear pants pocket

жопочник or **жопошник** (*zhopochnik* or *zhoposhnik*)—literally, *ass man*; a curse meaning homosexual

жопочка (*zhopochka*)—diminutive of **жопа** (*zhopa*), little ass

жопуля (*zhopulya*)—affectionate diminutive form of **жопа**

жопка (*zhopka*)—diminutive of *zhopa*

жопище (*zhopische*)—from *zhopa*, means *large ass*

жопа-помидор (*zhopa-pomidor*)—tomato ass, a shapely ass

жопа-апельсин (*zhopa-apel'sin*)—orange ass [the fruit, not the color], a shapely ass

жопа на колесах *(zhopa na kolyosakh)*—ass on wheels

жопа с ручой *(zhopa s ruchkoy)*—an ass with a handle on it

хитрая жопа *(hitraya zhopaya)*—smart-ass, crafty person

хитрожопый *(hitrozhopyi)*—ditto

Synonyms:

срака *(sraka)*—shitter (from срать *srat'*, to shit)

зад *(zad)*—rear end

задни ца *(zadnitsa)*—rear end

попа *(popa)*—behind

Popular expressions:

быть в глубокой жопе *(byt' v glubokoy zhope)*—literally, *to be in deep ass*, meaning to be in a difficult situation, in deep do-do/shit, up shit creek

в жопу пьяный *(v zhopu pyaniy)*—drunk off one's ass

дать по жопе *(dat' po zhope)*—to hit someone in the ass

брать за жопу *(brat' za zhopu)*—literally, *to take [someone] by the ass*, to catch, seize, arrest, catch red-handed

думать жопой *(dumat' zhopoy)*—literally, *to think with your ass*, meaning, to be stupid, make stupid decision, to have your head up your ass

искать на свою жопу приключений *(iskat' na svoyu zhopu priklyucheniyi)*—literally, *to look for adventures on your ass*, meaning to look for trouble, to take risks

поцелуй меня в жопу *(potselui menya v zhopu)*—kiss my ass

целовать в жопу *(tselovat' v zhopu)*—to kiss someone's ass

делать через жопу *(delat' cherez zhopu)*—to do things backward, stupidly, half-assedly

натяни глаз на жопу *(natyani glaz na zhopu)*—literally, *to pull someone's eye onto their ass*, meaning to beat the shit out of someone, to rearrange someone's face, to thrash someone, or to deceive someone

показать жопу *(pokazhat' zhopu)*—literally, *to show your ass*, meaning to refuse, to turn someone down flat

иметь в жопу *(imet' v zhopu)*—literally, *to get it in the ass*, to have sex, entering the partner from the rear, to be the active partner in anal sex

пристать как банный лист к жопе *(pristat' kak banniy list k zhope)*—literally, *to stick to someone like a bath leaf to their ass*, meaning to make a pest of oneself, to give someone no peace. Derived from the Russian bathhouse or sauna custom of beating oneself lightly with birch branches to purify the skin. In the damp hot atmosphere, the leaves then stick to the skin.

рвать на жопе волосы *(rvat' na zhope volosy)*—literally, *to pull out hairs on one's ass*, to be in despair or to regret, to tear one's hair out, to kick oneself

сравнить жопу с пальцем *(sravnit' zhopu s pal'tsem)*—literally, *to compare your ass with your finger*, meaning to compare unequal things, to compare apples and oranges

хоть жопой ешь! *(khot' zhopoy yesh'!)*—literally, *you could eat it with your ass*, meaning to have something to great excess, to have it coming out of your ears, to have shitloads of it

язык к жопе прилип *(yazyk k zhope prilip)*—literally, *[his] tongue stuck to his ass*, i.e., he has nothing to say, the cat got his tongue

Засунь себе в жопу! *(zasun' sebe v zhopu!)*—shove it up your ass!

Иди в жопу! *(Idi v zhopu)*—Go to the ass! Another place where Russians like to send people, as in "Go to hell!"

На каждую хитрую жопу есть хуй с винтом *(Na kazhduyu hitruyu zhopu est' huy s vintom)* Literally, *For every sly ass there is a prick with a screw*, meaning there is always somebody smarter than you are.

без мыла в жопу лезть (*bez myla v zhopu lest'*)—literally, *to crawl into someone's ass without soap,* meaning to be a toady, to brownnose

У тебя уже из жопы песок сыплется (*U tebya uzhe iz zhopy pesok sypletsya*)—literally, *you already have sand sprinkling out of your ass,* meaning, you're over the hill, you're no spring chicken

Dermo!

Хуй тебе в жопу! *(Huy tebe v zhopu!)* A prick up your ass! (a curse)

Шире жопы не пернешь. *(Shire zhopy ne pyornesh'.)* You can't fart wider than your ass—meaning there is a limit to everything.

Выше жопы не прыгнешь. *(Vyshe zhopy ne prygnesh'.)* Literally, *You can't jump higher than your ass*, meaning the same as above.

Нужен как зуб в жопе. *(Nuzhen kak zub v zhope.)* Literally, *I need that like I need a tooth in my ass*, meaning, I need that like a hole in the head; like a fish needs a bicycle.

жопа медом намазана *(zhopa myodom namazana)* Literally, *an ass spread with honey;* signifies something seductive. Example: **Что ты лезешь к ней? У неё что, жопа медом намазана?** *(Shto ty lezesh' k ney? U neyo shto, zhopa myodom namazana?)* Why are you always after her? Is her ass spread with honey, or what?

Еще посмотрим, чья жопа шире! *(Escho posmotrim chia zhopa shire!)* Literally, *We'll see whose ass is wider!* meaning, we'll see who the victor is, we'll see who comes out on top, who laughs last.

темно, как в жопе *(temno, kak v zhope)*—as dark as inside someone's ass: so dark you couldn't see your hand in front of your face

Здравствуй, жопа, новый год! *(Zdrastvui zhopa, novy gode!)* Hello, ass, happy New Year! (a joking greeting, signifying astonishment; well, I'll be goddamned!)

X

A Tour Through the Three Tiers of Russian Profanity

Вы ебали – не пропали
мы ебём, не пропадем!

Vy yebali-ne propali, my ebyom, ne propadyom!

You got laid and weren't afraid,
So we'll screw too, to hell with you!
—A son to his father

We studied this word a bit in the chapter entitled "Love-making, Russian Style." So without further ado, let's get right down to this activity's variations and numerous linguistic applications:

ебать *(yebat')*—to fuck

ебаться *(ebat'sya)*—to fuck, screw

ёбаный *(yobaniy)*—fucking (adjective)

ебанутый *(yebanuty)*—screwed-up

Dermo!

ебальник *(ebal'nik)*—literally, *fucker*, means mouth, kisser, "trap"

ебля *(eblya)*—intercourse, fucking

ебливый *(eblivy)*—liking to fuck, horny

В рот меня ебать! *(V rote menya ebat'!)*—an oath: May I be fucked in the mouth!

В рот тебя/её/его ебать! *(V rote tebya/eyo/evo ebat'!)*—a curse: Fuck you/her/him in the mouth!

ебать мозги *(ebat' mozgi)*—literally, *to brain fuck someone*, meaning to make someone sick of something, to annoy someone. Example: **Ну, пожалуйста, я тебя умоляю: перестань мне ебать мозги своими глупостямп!** *(Nu, pazhaluista, ya tebya umolyayu: perestan' mne ebat' mozgi svoimi glupostyami!)* Please, I beg of you, stop fucking my brains with your stupid ideas!

Ебут и фамилии не спрашивают. *(Ebut i familii ne sprashivayut.)*—literally, *they fuck without asking last names.* Means to act as one pleases, exploit people, force them to do things, etc.

еби их (вашу, твою) мать *(ebi ikh (vashu, tvoyu) mat')*—fuck their (your) mother

ёбнуть *(yobnut')*—to strike

наебать *(nayebat')*—to deceive

наебнуть *(nayebnut')*—1. to hit, strike; 2. to eat

выебать *(vyebat')*—1. to fuck; 2. to deceive, use

заебать *(zayebat')*—1. to fuck to utter exhaustion/to fuck one's brains out; 2. to make someone sick of something; 3. to say something without thinking

поебать (*poebat'*)—to fuck for a while

поёбывать (*poyobyvat'*)—to fuck from time to time

подъебнуть (*pod'ebnut'*)—to tease, taunt, to needle someone

приебаться (*priebat'sya*)—to make a pest of oneself with questions, requests, etc., to latch onto someone. Example: **Ну что ты приебался с этими вопросами?** (*Nu shto ty priebalsya s etimi voprosami?*) Why are you making a pest of yourself with your questions?

приёбываться (*priyobyvat'sya*)—provoke a fight, argument, clash

объебать (*ob'ebat'*)—to deceive

остоебенить (*ostoebenit'*)—to make someone sick of [something]

отъебать (*ot'ebat'*)—to fuck over

разъебай (*raz'ebi*)—a lackadaisical, unconscientious person

поебон (*poebon*)—copulation, often in the sense of an orgy; fuck-o-rama

поебушка (*poebushka*)—an informal get-together involving intercourse

Synonyms:

харить (*harit'*)—to get it on

жарить (*zharit'*)—literally, *to roast*

Факать (*fakat'*)—from the English word *fuck*

драть/отодрать (*drat'/otodrat'*)—literally, *to fight*, to tear to pieces, to thrash, flog

иметь (*imet'*)—literally, *to have*

употреблять (*upotreblyat'*)—literally, *to use*

сделать *(sdelat')*—literally, *to do it,* to do someone

заделать *(zadelat')*—literally, *to plug up a hole*

шворить *(shvorit')*

сношаться *(snoshat'sya)*—to have [sexual] relations, to copulate; can be either clinical or rude, depending on intonation.

Popular expressions:

Закрой ебало! *(Zakroy ebalo!)* Shut your trap!

ёбаный в рот *(yobaniy v rote)*—fucked in the mouth

ёбаный по кумполу *(yobani po kumpoly)*—fucked up in the head

Иди к ёбаной матери! *(Idi k yobanoi materi!)* Go to your fucking mother!—Russians' favorite place to tell people to go

Еби твою бога душу мать! *(Ebi tvoyu boga dushu mat'!)* Fuck your mother, soul of God!

ебёна мать *(ebyona mat')*—motherfucker; an all-purpose exclamation

Я его (тебя, её, вас) в рот ебал. *(Ya evo [tebya, eyo, vas] v rote yebal.)*—literally, *I fucked him* (you, her, you pl.) *in the mouth,* meaning I don't give a damn about him, I don't give a flying fuck about you.

ебитская сила *(ebitskaya sila)*—literally, *fucking strength,* an exclamation signifying astonishment, something like the English expressions *Holy shit! Well, fuck me! I'll be goddamned!*

Now that you are at least partially acquainted with the glories of real Russian speech, you can practice building multitiered constructions of Russian expletives all by yourself. It's very simple to do (using prefixes, suffixes, and case endings). For example, take three words: **хуй, пизда**, and **ебать**. Look what you get if you stack them up the way children stack building blocks:

1. **хуем ебаная пизда** *(huyem yobanaya pizda)*—prick-fucked cunt (This is primitive; the very simplest level.)

2. **хуем пизданутый ебака** *(huyem pizdanuty yebaka)*—a fucker pussywhipped by a prick (This is getting more interesting.)

3. **ёбаный в пизду хуй** *(yobani v pizdu huy)*—a prick fucked in the cunt (This is enigmatic.)

4. **на хуй припиздяченная ебля** *(na huy pripizdyachennaya yeblia)*—cunted-nearly-to-death pricked fucking (Now, this is *real* triple-decker profanity.)

Now you can practice yourself, for the Russian language gives unlimited opportunities to do so. The more you practice, the more convinced you will become that the Russian language is indeed a mighty one.

An Additional Alphabetical Glossary
of Real Russian, Which Is Far
from Complete

A.

А пошел ты! (к черту, к лешему, в жопу, к ебёной матери, и,пр.) *(A poshel ty! [k chortu, k leshemu, v zhopu, k yebyonay materi,* etc.])) Oh, go on with you! Get outta here! Go to the devil/to hell/to the ass/motherfucker!

аборт *(abort)* abortion

адюльтер, иметь адюльтер *(adyulter, imet' adyulter)* to have sexual relations with a woman

акт половой *(akt polovoy)* the sex act

алименты *(alimenty)* child support

аллах с ним! *(allakh s nim!)* the hell with him!

амба *(amba)* fiasco, flop

атанда! *(atanda!)* attention!

Атас *(Atas)* Heads up! Someone's coming!

Б.

бадяга, бадягу разводить *(badyaga, badyagu razvodit')* to shoot the breeze, to shoot the shit

базар *(bazar)* conversation, confabulation, bull session

базлать *(bazlat')* to raise Cain, to raise hell, to have a ruckus or a blowup

баки, забивать баки, травить баки *(baki, zabivat' baki, travit' baki)* to weave a yarn, prevaricate, fib

балбес *(balbes)* dunderhead

бандерша *(bandersha)* procuress, madame of a bordello

барать / бараться *(barat' / barat'sya)* to fuck, to bang [in the sense of *fuck*]

бардак *(bardak)* whorehouse; junk, mess

баруха *(barukha)* strumpet

барыга *(baryga)* a trafficker in stolen, hot or fenced goods

барышня *(baryshyna)* lass, girl

башли *(bashli)* dough, money

баки, бочата *(baki, bochata)* clock, watch

батя *(batya)* father, Daddy

бздун *(bzdun)* wimp, chicken, coward

блат *(blat)* clout, connection, pull or influence

блуд *(blud)* debauchery, promiscuity

белый танец *(bely tanets)* a dance in which women invite men to dance/Sadie Hawkins Dance; literally, *white dance*

беременность *(beremennost')* pregnancy

бешенство матки *(beshenstvo matki)* nymphomania, literally, *uterine madness*

болт *(bolt)* tool, as in *penis*

бордель *(bordel')* bordello

брать на понт *(brat' na pont)* to pull someone's leg

брать на горло *(brat' na gorlo)* to bellow orders at someone

брать на лапу *(brat' na lapu)* to have one's palm greased, to receive a bribe

брюхо *(bryukho)* belly

брюхатая баба *(bryukhataya baba)* a woman who's been knocked up/is preggers

буфера *(bufera)* knockers, boobs

бяка *(byaka)* an icky person

В.

вамп *(vamp)* predatory woman

венерик / венеричка *(venerik / venerichka)* someone with venereal disease (m.,f.)

вертихвостка *(vertikhvostka)* an ass-swinger, hussy

вздрючка *(vzdryuchka)* taking someone to task, cussing out

взъёбка *(vzyobka)* a bawling-out, a reading of the riot act to someone

взасос целоваться *(vzasos tselovat'sya)* to suck face, French kiss

влопаться *(vlopat'sya)* to have a thing for someone, a crush on someone

влюбиться по уши *(vlyubit'sya po ushi)* to fall head over heels in love; literally, *to fall in love up to one's ears*

вонь *(von')* stink, stench

вонять *(vonyat')* to stink

втюриться *(vtyurit'sya)* to get a crush on

втрескаться *(vtreskat'sya)* to go gaga over someone

вставать *(vstavat')* to stand up, get erect, get hard, get a hard-on

выблядок *(vyblyadok)* son of a whore

выебать *(vyebat')* to fuck

выёбываться *(vyobyvat'sya)* to swagger, show off

выпендриваться *(vypendrivat'sya)* to parade oneself, show off, get fancy ideas about one's own importance

вхуячить *(vhuyachit')* to hit someone, give them a thrashing

Г.

г . . . *(g . . .)* euphemism for *govno*, shit; used in books

гад *(gad)* louse, skunk, rat

гинеколог *(ginekolog)* gynecologist

говно *(govno)* shit

говноёб *(govnoyob)* a wishy-washy person; literally, *shit-eater*

гомик *(gomik)* homo

Д.

декрет *(dekret)* maternity leave

Дело в шляпе. *(Delo v shlyape.)* It's a done deal, we have it in the bag; literally, *The deal is in the hat.*

динамо *(dinamo)* the name of a popular sports league in Russia

динамо *(dinamo)* a woman who parties at a man's expense and leads him on, but then avoids settling accounts through sex and refuses to put out; a cock tease, prick tease

долдон *(doldon)* dunderhead

дока *(doka)* a whiz, a maven

донжуанский список *(donzhuansky spisok)* body count, i.e., a list of the women a man has slept with, literally, *Don Juan list*

доска *(doska)* flat-chested woman, washboard; literally, *board*

в доску пьян, в сиську пьян, в жопу пьян *(v dosku pyan/v sis'ku pyan, v zhopu pyan)* drunk off his ass, plastered, shitfaced, messed up

доступная женщина *(dostupnaya zhenshchina)* an easy lay; literally, *available woman*

дрочить *(drochit')* to jerk off, to wank off

дурь *(dur')* dope, i.e., drugs

Ё.

Ёлки-палки! / Ёлки-моталки! *(Yolkki-palki!/Yolki-motalki!)* For crying out loud! Jeepers creepers!

Ж.

ж . . . *(zh . . .)* euphemism for *zhopa*, ass; used in books

жопа *(zhopa)* ass

жарить *(zharit')* to have sex, to get it on

же *(zhe)* sign in women's public toilets

жених *(zhenikh)* bridegroom or fiancé

женихаться *(zhenikhat'sya)* to act like a bridegroom

жить с кем-то *(zhit' s kem-to)* to live with someone; i.e., to have sex with someone

3.

завалить в кровать *(zavalit' v krovat')* to get/tumble someone into bed, to take a tumble with someone, a roll in the hay

завязать *(zavyazat')* to put a halt to something, to cut it out

зад, задница *(zad, zadnitsa)* rear end, bottom

задний проход *(zadniy prokhod)* rear entry, i.e., anus

заебать в доску *(zayebat' v dosku)* to fuck your brains out

заебать до смерти *(zayebat' do smerti)* to fuck to death

заебать на хуй *(zayebat' na huy)* to fuck like a maniac

зажигающая баба *(zazhigayuschaya baba)* a hot babe, hot to trot

закидоны *(zakidony)* outbursts, strange actions, hang-ups

закрутить любовь *(zakrutit' lyubov')* to make time with someone, to get a courtship underway

залупа *(zalupa)* foreskin

зараза *(zaraza)* You vile creature! literally, *infection*

засадить *(zasadit')* to fuck, to stick it in

засандалить *(zasandalit')* same as above

засранец *(zasranets)* filthy creature; literally, *someone who soils things with shit*

захуячить *(zahuyachit')* to do something (based on the root **хуй** *(huy)* meaning dick, cock)

захуярить *(zahuyarit')* same as above

зверь-мужик *(zver-muzhik)* sex-machine, someone who is tireless in bed

зек *(zek)* convict, prisoner, jailbird, inmate

И.

иди в задницу *(idi v zadnitsu)* go to hell; literally, *go to butt*

иди в жопу *(idi v zhopu)* go to ass

иди на хуй *(idi na huy)* go to dick

иди в пизду *(idi v pizdu)* go to cunt

иди к ебаной матери *(idi k yebanoy materi)* go to motherfucker

иди к черту *(idi k chortu)* go to the devil

иди на фиг *(idi na fig)* get outta here!

иди ты *(idi ty)* go on!

иди к шутам *(idi k shutam)* go to the wiseguys

иди знаешь куда *(idi znaesh' kuda)* you know where you should go

идиот *(idiot)* idiot

К.

кадр *(kadr)* chick, female

кадрёж *(kadryozh)* a flirt/a tease

кадрить *(kadrit')* to flirt, bat one's eyelashes at

какого рожна *(kakovo rozhna)* what the hell

кантоваться *(kantovat'sya)* to do nothing and pretend you are working, or to spend time waiting for something—but **не кантовать!** *(ne kantovat'!)* means not to bother someone

катись отсюда *(katis' otsyuda)* make tracks, get outta here, make yourself scarce, split

Катись к ёбаной матери на легком катере! *(Katis' k yobanoy materi na lekhkom katere!)* Go to hell in a steamboat! [rhymes in the original]

качать права *(kachat' prava)* to stand up for/assert one's rights; literally, *to pump one's rights*

качель, туды его в качель *(kachel', tudy evo v kachel')* go take a walk

кемарить *(kemarit')* to conk out, hit the sack

киркнуть / кирять *(kirknut' / kiryat')* to tipple, to wet one's whistle, to hit the bottle

классный кадр *(klassny kadr)* a class act [said of a sexy woman]

климакс *(klimaks)* change of life, menopause

кобель *(kobel')* a man who fucks a lot, a stud

козел *(kozyol)* goat [insult]

кончать *(konchat')* to come

кот / котяря *(kot / kotyara)* a man who changes women regularly, a tomcat

красуля *(krasulya)* a pretty woman

крутить яйца *(krutit' yaytsa)* to get on someone's nerves; literally, *to twist someone's balls*

крутить жопой *(krutit' zhopoy)* to twitch one's ass, i.e., to flirt

крыша *(krysha)* patron, protector from criminals or police

крыша поехала *(krysha poekhala)* [someone] went bonkers

курица *(kuritsa)* chick, babe; literally, *chicken*

Л.

лабух *(labuhk)* jazzman

лажа *(lazha)* baloney, as in nonsense

лапать *(lapat')* to grope [a woman]

лахудра *(lakhudra)* a hooker

лезть на рожон *(lezt' na rozhon)* to go looking for trouble

лимон *(limon)* a cool million

лифчик *(lifchick)* bra

лыбиться *(lybit'sya)* to crack a smile

любовник *(lyubovnik)* lover (m.)

любовница *(lyubovnitsa)* lover (f.), mistress

любодейство *(lyubodaystvo)* physical love, the sex act

лярва *(lyarva)* fast woman

М.

малофья *(malofya)* come (also spelled *cum*), meaning sperm

манда *(manda)* cunt, pussy

мандавошка *(mandavoshka)* pubic louse [term of invective]

материть *(materit')* to curse

матерщина *(materschina)* four-letter words, swearwords, expletives, profanities

мать-перемать *(mat'-peremat)* fuck your mother twice over

мегера *(megera)* a homely person, a real dog

милёнок *(milyonok)* a sweet guy

мильтон *(mil'ton)* militiaman, cop, fuzz

минет *(minet)* oral sex

минетчица *(minetzhitsa)* a woman who gives head, cocksucker, fellatrix

мудохать *(mudokhat')* to fart around

Н.

На кой леший? *(Na koy leshiy)* Why on earth?

На кой пес? *(Na koy pes?)* Whatever for?

нужда малая *(nuzhda malaya)* number one [urination]

нужда большая *(nuzhda bol'shaya)* number two [defecation]

нужник *(nuzhnik)* john, the can, toilet

Ну тебя к черту! *(Nu tebya k chortu!)* To hell with you!

О.

онанист *(onanist)* masturbator, jerk-off, wanker

оргазм *(orgasm)* orgasm

остоебенить *(ostoyebenit')* to make someone sick and tired of you

отвешивать пиздюлей *(otveshivat' pizdulay)* to beat, to give a drubbing

отдаваться *(otdavat'sya)* to give oneself [to someone], i.e., to have sex

отодрать *(otodrat')* to fuck

отпиздить *(otpizdit')* to beat, to pummel

отпиздярить (*otpizdyarit'*) to beat, to batter

отпиздячить (*otpizdyachit'*) to beat, to trounce

отхуячить (*othuyachit'*) to beat, to mash

отфуячить (*otfuyachit'*) to beat, to wallop

отхуярить (*othuyarit'*) to beat, to give it to someone

отхарить (*otharit'*) to fuck with relish, to get it on

отшить (*otsheet'*) to get rid of someone, to send them packing

отодрать (*otodrat'*) to get rid of someone, to slough someone off

отхватить бабу, мужчину (*otkhvatit' babu, muzhschiny*) to get a girl, to catch a man

отъебаться / Отьебись! (*ot'yebat'sya / Ot'ebis'!*) to fuck off, Fuck off!

охуеть (*ohuyet'*) to go nuts/to be thrilled, impressed

охуительно (*ohuyitel'no*) amazing, wonderful

очко (*ochko*) asshole

П.

паршивка / паршивец (*parshivka / parshivets*) urchin (m., f.)

пах (*pakh*) crotch, groin

пацан (*patsan*) shaver, small fry, whippersnapper, little boy

пахан (*pakhan*) godfather, gang leader

педераст (*pederast*) homosexual

педик (*pedik*) faggot, queer

пердила (*perdila*) lunk, large man; literally, *big fart*

пипка (*pipka*) cuntlet (little cunt)

пипочка (*pipochka*) same as above

пиписька (*pipis'ka*) same as above

пизда (*pizda*) cunt

пиздой накрыться (*pizdoy nakryt'sya*) to be a total loss, a total waste, a washup

пизду смешить (*pizdu smeshit'*) to screw around, screw up

Пошел в пизду! *(Poshul v pizdu!)* Go to hell! literally, *go to cunt*

пиздюлей навтыкать, дать *(pizdyulay navtykat', dat')* to punch someone in the face

пиздострадатель *(pizdostradatel')* cunt-sufferer, sexually frustrated man in search of satisfaction, sex maniac

пистон поставить *(piston postavit')* to have a one-night stand with someone; literally, *to stick the piston in,* to insert the piston

Плевать я хотел! *(Plevat' ya hotel!)* I couldn't care less! [I don't give a damn!]; literally, *I felt like spitting!*

показать где раки зимуют *(pokazat' gde raki zimuyut)* show [someone] what's what, give someone what for; literally, *show* [someone] *where the crayfish [spend the] winter*

попиздеть *(popizdet')* shoot the shit, shoot the bull

попиздюхать *(popizdyukhat')* to go, to vamoose

послать к бабушке *(poslat' k babushke)* literally, *to send somebody to grandmother,* i.e., to send someone packing

Пососи! *(Pososi!)* Suck on it! meaning, fat chance! Yeah, that plus a dollar fifty will get you a ride on the New York subway!

потаскуха *(potaskukha)* trollop

похабщина *(pokhabschina)* cussing, foul language

прибарахлиться *(pribarakhlit'sya)* to get dolled up/decked out/gussied up/tarted up

прилипать *(prilipat')* to make a pass at someone

поехать в ригу *(poekhat' v rigu)* to throw up, pray to the porcelain god; literally, *to go to riga*

Р.

развратник *(razvratnik)* pervert

распутник *(rasputnik)* lech, dirty old man

разъебай / разпиздяй *(raz'ebaye / razpizdyaye)* fuck-up, someone who botches things, makes a hash of things

рожа кирпича просит *(rozha kirpicha prosit)* an ugly person; literally, *his face is just asking for a brick*

Руки прочь! *(Ruki proch'!)* Hands off!

C.

сабантуй *(sabantui)* party, shindig; also, a prison uprising

самец *(samets)* male animal, stallion, buck, etc., applied to men, meaning *real man*, etc.

сачковать *(sachkovat')* to play hooky from work

сбацать *(sbatstat')* to bang or strum on a musical instrument

свалиться с катушек *(svalist'sya s katushek)* to fall head over heels

свист *(svist)* tall tale, lie; literally, *whistle*

сексопильная *(seksopil'naya)* sexy, having sex appeal, a real babe

симпатяга *(simpatyaga)* sweet guy

сказал как в лужу пёрнул *(skazal kak v luzhu pyornul)* to commit a faux pas, say something that stops everyone in their tracks by its inappropriateness or stupidity; literally, *to say something as if farting in a puddle*

слабак *(slabak)* weakling, wimp

Слабо! *(Slabo!)* I dare you! **Не слабо!** *(Ne slabo!)* Not bad! Super!

Не слабо ты меня надул, падла! *(Ne slabo ty menya nadul, padla!)* Well I be damned if you didn't do a number on me!

сношаться *(snoshat'sya)* to fuck, to rut, to copulate

сношение *(snosheniye)* mating

строить глазки *(stroit' glazki)* to make eyes at

сучка *(suchka)* a real bitch

сожитель *(sozhitel')* live-in lover/common-law spouse

спирохет *(spirokhet)* worm, noodle, a weak, skinny man, not worth noticing

спустить *(spustit')* to come, to shoot one's wad

стебанутый *(styobanuty)* nuts, crazy, flipped out. Example: **джазухой стебанутый** *(djazzukhoy styobanuty)* nuts about jazz

стучать *(stuchat')* to rat on someone, inform

Сука буду-не забуду. *(Suka budu-ne zabudu.)* I'll be a bitch—I won't forget. [saying, oath, like the English expression *Cross my heart and hope to die / stick a needle in my eye.*]

Т.

теща *(tyescha)* mother-in-law

темнить *(temnit')* to beat around the bush, lie or hide something

тискать *(tiskat')* fondle, grope

титьки *(tit'ki)* tits

толкать *(tolkat')* to move [goods], to peddle, to hawk, to unload, to sell

травить *(travit')* to throw up, lose your lunch; also, to lie

трахнуть / трахаться *(trakhnut' / trakhat'sya)* to fuck

трепло *(treplo)* a blowhard, braggart

трепаться *(trepat'sya)* to brag

триппер *(tripper)* the clap, gonorrhea

труба-дело *(truba-delo)* the game's up

туфта *(tufta)* humbug, gimmick, racket, deception

У.

убивец *(ubivets)* rod, penis of lethal proportions, from **убить** *(ubit')*, meaning *to kill*

ублюдок *(ublyudok)* a cur, a mongrel, a miscreant

удавка *(udavka)* necktie; literally, *noose*

усраться можно (от смеха) *(usrat'sya mozhno)* *(ot*

smekha) it's enough to make you split your sides, to be in stitches; literally, *to shit from laughing so hard*

утка *(utka)* bedpan; literally, *duck*

Ф.

факаться *(fakat'sya)* to fuck [borrowed from English]

фаловать *(falovat')* to give something the hard sell, to talk into

фарцовщик *(fartsovschik)* black marketeer who deals in foreign goods

феня *(fenya)* underworld lingo, slang for *talk the talk*

фига *(figa)* zilch

Фиг с ней / с ним. *(Fig s nay / s nim.)* The heck / the hell with her / with him.

фигня *(fignya)* hot air, balderdash

фигли-мигли *(figli-migli)* hanky-panky, fraud, chicanery

филон *(filon)* loafer, layabout, lazy lug

филонить *(filonit')* to look busy while actually doing nothing

фраер *(fryer)* a sucker, someone who is not initiated into the ways of the criminal world

фря *(frya)* social climber

фуй *(fuy)* euphemism for *huy*, meaning *dick, cock*

фуфло *(fuflo)* bogus, fake

Х.

халява *(halyava)* freebie

хахаль *(hahal')* paramour

хер *(hair)* prick, dick, cock

на хер *(na hair)* to the devil

На кой хер! *(Na koy hair!)* What the fuck!

ни хера *(ni haira)* chickenshit, peanuts, something piddling

Ни хера себе! *(Ni haira sebya!)* Well, I'll be fucked!

херовина *(herovina)* thingamajig

хреновина *(hrenovina)* whatchamacallit

химичить *(himichit')* con, swindle, take for a ride

хлять / хилять *(hylat' / hilyat')* to masquerade as

хмырь *(hmyr')* shady character

ходок *(hodok)* Romeo, a tomcat

хохмить *(hohmit')* to banter, to wisecrack

хуё-моё *(huyo-moyo)* whatever, whatnot, blah blah blah and so on

хуёвина *(huyovina)* stuff, thing, thingamajig

хуем груши окалачивать *(huyem grushi okalachivat')* to contemplate one's navel; literally, *to hit pear trees with one's cock*

Ц.

целка *(tselka)* untouched, intact (virgin)

цирлы *(tsirli)* tippy-toes

цицка *(tsitska)* titties

Ч.

червонец *(chervonets)* ten [rubles], tenner, ten spot

четвертак *(chetvertak)* twenty-five

чертыхаться *(chertykhat'sya)* to swear using the word **черт** *(chort)* devil

чехвостить *(chekhvostit')* to talk dirty

член *(chlen)* penis

чувак *(chuvak)* dude

чувиха *(chuvikha)* babe

Ш.

шестерка *(shestyorka)* sidekick, gofer

шибздик *(shibzdik)* ninety-eight-pound weakling

ширинка *(shirinka)* fly [of the pants]

шлында *(shlynda)* groupie, bimbo

шнобель *(shnobel')* schnozz, big nose

штучки-дрючки *(shtuchki-dryuchki)* hanky-panky, fraud, chicanery, skulduggery

Я.

ядрёна мать *(yadrona mat')* motherfucker

ядрёна вошь *(yadrona vosh')* louse-fucker

ядрёна мышь *(yadrona mysh')* mouse-fucker

яйца *(yaytsa)* balls [testicles]; **морочить яйца** *(morochit' yaytsa)* fool around, mix up; **чесать яйца** *(chesat' yaytsa)* literally, to scratch one's balls, i.e., to sit around doing nothing, twiddle one's thumbs; **слону яйца качать** *(slonu yaytsa kachat')* literally, to bat an elephant's balls back and forth, to sit around doing nothing, to stare at one's navel, twiddle one's thumbs

A Brief Glossary of Essential English Terms Accompanied by Russian Translations

ass	жопа	*zhopa*
bitch	сука	*suka*
boobs, knockers	буфера	*buffera*
cocksucker	хуесоска	*huyesoska*
cunt	пизда	*pizda*
damn it	черт побери	*chort poberi*
dick	хуй	*huy*
faggot	педик	*pedik*
fool	дурак	*durak*
for crying out loud	ёлки-палки	*yolki-palki*
fuck	ебать	*ebat'*
fuck off	отьебись	*ot'yebis*
go to hell	иди к черту	*idi k chortu*

jerk	хер моржовый	*hair morzhovy*
to jerk off	дрочить	*drochit'*
motherfucker	ёб твою мать	*yobe tvoyu mat'*
pervert	извращенец	*izvraschenets*
pig	свинья	*svinya*
pimp	сутенёр	*sutenyor*
prick	хуй	*huy*
prostitute	проститутка	*prostitutka*
pussy	манда	*manda*
rape	изнасилование	*iznasilovaniye*
screw you	едри твою мать	*edri tvoyu mat'*
sexual harassment	сексуальное домогательство	*seksual'noye domogatel'stvo*
shit	говно, дерьмо	*govno, der'mo*
shithead	говнюк	*govnyuk*
slut/whore	блядь	*blyad'*
son of a bitch	сукин сын	*sukin syn*
Stop farting around!	Перестань мудохаться!	*Perestan' mudokhat'sya!*
wimp	слабак	*slabak*